How to Answer Dumb Dating Questions

How to Answer Dumb Dating Questions

Creative & tested responses to those difficult dating questions.
Keep your sanity, weed out the crazies and find Mr. Right.

India Kang

With a foreword by Ellen Fein and Sherrie Schneider
#1 *New York Times* bestselling authors of *The Rules*.

YOUCAXTON PUBLICATIONS
OXFORD & SHREWSBURY

Copyright © India Kang 2017

The author asserts the moral right to
be identified as the author of this work.

ISBN 978-1-911175-67-4
Printed and bound in Great Britain & USA.
Published by YouCaxton Publications 2017

All rights reserved. No part of this publication may be reproduced, stored in a retrieval system, or transmitted in any form or by any means, electronic, mechanical, photocopying, recording or otherwise, without the prior permission of the publisher.

This book is sold subject to the condition that it shall not, by way of trade or otherwise, be lent, resold, hired out or otherwise circulated without the publisher's prior consent in any form of binding or cover other than that in which it is published and without a similar condition including this condition being imposed on the subsequent purchaser.

YouCaxton Publications
enquiries@youcaxton.co.uk

Contents

Foreword — ix
Preface — x
Introduction — xi
Disclaimer — xii
How This Book Works — xiii

PART ONE
DATING QUESTIONS DURING THE DATE SET UP

1. Guiding Him to Ask for Your Number Online — 3
2. What to Do If He Has Your Number and Doesn't Call Straight Away — 8
3. What to Do If He Asks for Your Number on Chat or Instant Messenger — 9
4. How to Move the Conversation on from Email to Phone — 11
5. How to Move the Conversation on from Text to Calls — 13
6. How to Reply to Common Texts or Emails — 14
7. How to Get Him to Call at a Time Convenient for You — 18
8. How to Guide Him to Ask for Your Number in Person — 19
9. What If He Asks for Your Number But You're Not Interested? — 21
10. Why Do Men Ask Personal Questions Straight Away? — 22
11. What to Do If He Ends the Message with 'x' in the Form of a Kiss — 23
12. How to End the Call First — 24
13. How to Manage Questions About Facebook — 25
14. How to Keep Your Privacy While Dating — 27
Case Study — 29

PART TWO
QUESTIONS ASKED DURING THE DATING PROCESS

1. How to Respond to Common Texts and Emails — 33
2. "Is Now a Good Time to Talk?" — 35
3. He Texts: "Looking Forward to Seeing You Tomorrow" — 36
Case Study — 37
4. He Says: "Let Me Know a Good Time to Call?" — 38
5. He Asks: "How Come You Don't Text?" — 40
Case Study: If I'm on a Date and He Asks If I'm Seeing Anyone Else. — 42
6. He Asks: "What's with the Two Word Text Responses?" — 44
7. He Asks: "Are You on Skype? We Could Skype?" — 45
8. He Asks: "Do You IM or Whatsapp?" — 46
9. "What Are Your Plans for the Weekend?" — 48
10. He Says: "I See You're Divorced or Separated" — 49
11. He Asks: "Have You Dated Much?" — 51
12. He Asks: "Are You Dating Anyone Else?" — 52
13. He Asks: "Are You Even Interested in Me?" — 53
14. "What Are You Looking for in a Man?" — 54

15	He Asks: "What's Your Ideal Man?"	55
16	He Asks: "What Time Do You Finish Work?"	57
17	"Fancy a Hook Up?"	58
18	He Asks: "Do You Have Any Dating Stories?"	59
19	He Says: "Tell Me About Yourself?"	61
20	He Says: "Tell Me Three Things About Yourself?"	62
21	He Asks: "How Long Have You Been Single?"	63
22	He Asks "How Do You Find This Whole Dating Scene?"	64
23	He Asks: "Is There Anywhere You'd Like to Go?"	65
24	"Are You Still Ok for Tonight?"	66
25	"What's the Plan for Tonight?"	67
26	"Hey, I'm Thinking of Going to a Movie, Any Interest?"	69
27	He Asks: "Are You Free Tonight?"	70
28	"Are You Willing to Relocate?"	71
29	How to Respond to Cutesy Messages	72
30	Why Do Men Send Random Messages and What Do They Mean?	73
31	He Called, We Had a Great Chat, and He Didn't Ask Me Out. What Do I Do?	74
32	A Guy I Met Online Has Called Five Times. I Keep Missing His Calls. Should I Text Him Back?	75
33	What to Do If He Texts and Calls, Yet Never Arranges Date Plans	76
	Case Study	77
	Case Study	78
34	How to Organise a Date Via Text	79
35	Why Some Men Don't Arrange Date Plans	82
36	We Have a Date in the Diary, It's Getting Close and He Hasn't Confirmed! Should I Make Other Plans?	84
37	What to Do If He Postpones the Date Time	86
38	We Met Online; I Don't Feel Safe Getting into His Car. Help!	87

PART THREE
IN BETWEEN DATES

1	How to Make Him Pay for Dates	91
2	What to Do If He Tries to Prolong the Date	93
3	If He Wants to See You Again and You Don't Want Another Date	94
4	What to Do If Your Date Arrives Late	95
5	If He Doesn't Call, Should I Call Him?	96
6	How to Navigate the 'Exclusivity Chat'	97
7	Why Hasn't He Deleted His Online Dating Profile?	99
8	I Checked His Profile, He's Still Active Online. What Should I Do?	101

PART FOUR
LEADING UP TO AND ONCE EXCLUSIVE

1	If You Can't Make a Date, Can You Suggest Alternative Days?	105
2	Can I Ever Call Him?	106
3	What If He Thinks I'm Not Interested?	108
4	How to Help Him Lead	109

5	How to Navigate Cooking	110
6	Do You Assume You Have a Date on Saturday and Tolerate Late Details?	112
7	I'm on WhatsApp. He Can See When I'm Online. How Do I Navigate?	113
8	If I Delete His Number, How Will I Know It's Him?	115
9	Some Other Common Messages and How to Respond	116
	Case Study	121

PART FIVE
HANDLING QUESTIONS AROUND MARRIAGE, CHILDREN AND PAST RELATIONSHIPS

1	Questions Related to Marriage	125
2	He Asks "Do You Want Children?"	127
3	Questions About Past Relationships	129
4	How to Navigate the Ex	132

PART SIX
SOME COMMON *RULES* FURTHER EXPLAINED

1	Wednesday for Saturday and the Three Day *Rule*	138
2	How to Navigate Last-Minute Dates	139
3	How to Make Him Travel to You	140
4	How to Successfully Navigate the Meeting-Halfway *Rule*	141
	Case Study	144
	Case Study	145
5	How to Navigate the Dead Zone	146
6	What Is the Date Zero?	147
7	Bookmarking	149

PART SEVEN
ODDS AND ENDS BUT STILL IMPORTANT

1	Why Do Men Only Talk About Themselves?	153
2	Men Who Ask Interview-type Questions	155
3	I Don't Need a Man	156
4	The Dating Phone	157
5	What to Do If You're Propositioned?	158
6	What Are You Up To?	159
7	You vs. Non-*Rules* Girls	160
	Case Study	163
	Case Study	164
	Case Study	166
	Case Study	167

About India Kang	168
Information and Resources You Can Use:	169

Foreword

We know dating can be tough. We know it's not easy, which is why we wrote the original *Rules I* and *II* together with *Not Your Mother's Rules*. India Kang understands this too. Follow the advice in this book and so will you!

India Kang provides answers to all those difficult dating questions. Reading this book will give you clarity and insight into why men ask the questions they do. Plus, India tells you exactly what to do and how to respond.

Thanks to India Kang, the perfect responses to all those difficult dating questions are now at your fingertips.

Don't set up another date until you've read and re-read this book. We say after you've read our books, you MUST read India Kang's book to navigate through dating!

Ellen Fein and Sherrie Schneider
#1 *New York Times* bestselling authors of *The Rules*

Preface

Whether you're online dating, using dating apps, speed dating or have a blind date, you'll always get asked a number of questions. Don't shy away from these questions. Embrace them and use this book to help master the answers.

Questions are completely natural. They're a way for someone to get to know you better.

And, while I don't feel men ask 'trick' questions, the reality is your responses can either raise or lower your dating credentials. The aim of this book is to give you the dating edge.

This book is intended for anyone who is currently dating and searching for Mr. Right. If you've ever wondered *"how do I respond when he asks?"* then this book is for you.

The good news is that the majority of men ask the same questions. Once you've practiced the answers a few times, responding to his questions becomes a breeze.

I know from personal experience how tough urban dating can be. I also know that with some work, persistence and patience it does work. Refuse to give up and you will definitely find your personal Mr. Right.

I hope you find this book useful and I hope the answers help smooth your dating journey.

If you can't find the answer to your question or dilemma, get in touch via *www.indiakang.com*

Now, please get out there and date.

Introduction

The advice in this book is based on *The Rulesbook* philosophy by the bestselling authors Ellen Fein and Sherrie Schneider. All the answers outlined in this book are tried, tested and proven to work.

No matter where you live and regardless of your background or culture, when it comes to urban dating the majority of men ask the same dating questions.

Why do they do it? Who knows! Don't fight it.

Get one step ahead of the game. The tried and tested knowledge in this book, will help you answer those difficult dating questions, and help you navigate the dating jungle.

Since, it's not all about what you say, but also the way you say it, some of the responses are accompanied with either a 'note,' or 'tone.' This is to help guide you on how to deliver your responses.

Wishing you lots of dating success and happiness.

India Kang x

Disclaimer

If you're not comfortable with the philosophy of *The Rulesbook*, and if you don't feel it's a man's job to ask for dates, pick you up and pay, then this book is not for you.

This book is based on the premise that men and women are biologically different. While women control the emotional and spiritual aspects of a relationship, when it comes to dating and romance the man leads.

This does not make women weak and inferior. Far from it. If you understand the timeless teachings of *The Rulesbook*, you'll know that, among other things, the teachings are about dating with respect and dignity, weeding out the time wasters and loving those who love you. The goal of this book isn't to pretend to be someone you're not, but rather to keep the ball in your court.

If you're looking for a committed and fulfilling relationship and want to find your perfect Mr. Right while weeding out the crazies, please read on.

How This Book Works

Dating is a process and can take a lot of work. Truthfully, you need to treat finding "The One" as if it were a full-time job.

This book reflects the different dating stages and is split into seven sections, to help you navigate questions asked during the different stages:

- Setting up the date.

- Actually on the date.

- In the time between dates.

- Exclusive with one man.

- Handling questions around marriage, children and past relationships.

- Some common *Rules* further explained.

- Odds and ends, but still important.

While the answers in this book are suggestions only, they are based on tested dating wisdom and work in the vast majority of cases.

Remember — if you're practicing *The Rules,* nothing bad happens because you miss one text or one call. The world doesn't end. At worst, you've weeded out a time waster. At best, he gets to chase you. All good!

I've also included answers to some commonly asked dating questions. Again, if you have a question which isn't answered in this book, please do get in touch via the website www.indiakang.com.

Finally, I recommend taking some time to practice the answers in this book. You'll find most men ask the same questions. Master the answers in this book, raise your dating game and live happily ever after.

PART ONE

DATING QUESTIONS DURING THE DATE SET UP

1

Guiding Him to Ask for Your Number Online

This will take one of several forms. When dating online or via apps, lots of men add their personal email address and number at the end of their first or second email.

The message may read along the lines of:

Hey, I saw your profile and noticed you like skydiving. Me too! Fancy a skydive together?
Matt
matt@googlemail.com
07654 423 678

Why Do Men Do This?

He is trying to make things easier by putting the ball in your court. He's saying he is interested. He counts this as making the first move and hopes you'll call.

Why Can't He Ask for My Number Already?

He doesn't know he has to. The dating scene is constantly changing and he's being cautious. He doesn't want to offend you. He is concerned about coming across as too forward by asking for your number. Maybe he annoyed some girls by asking for their number 'too soon'. He doesn't want you to think he's moving too fast, and thinks you might prefer to email first.

So yes, he's playing it safe. Cut him some slack. He can't read your mind and doesn't know you want him to ask. This doesn't make him a loser! He's trying his best and working out which way works.

Don't fret, here are a few ways to navigate the number exchange process.

You can respond back with:

Option one: the no-nonsense approach

"Great I'm on 07658 143 256."

And that's it. Simply give him your number or email. Now it's up to him to call. After getting your number the vast majority of men will text.

Some men think that by texting first, they are being polite. Remember you set the boundaries. If you text back immediately, he'll come to expect an immediate response. You must wait four hours before texting back.

Some men may text and say:
"Let me know a good time to call?"

The best way to respond, is to text with:
"Hey, any time is cool. Speak soon."
This gives him an open window to call whenever he likes.
If you say:
"Hey, evenings between 7pm and 9pm are great."
What usually happens, is that you get into a text fest right away. Typically, he won't wait until 7 o'clock. Instead he will probably text back:
"Are you free now?"
The reason he does this, is because, he knows your phone is in your hand right now. The reason he knows that, is because you've just texted him. They're smart!

To avoid any backwards and forwards texting, there are two tried and tested options:

1. Ignore his text and wait for him to call.
2. Respond with: *"Hey, whenever suits you is fine. Speak soon."*

By replying in this way, he's free to call whenever he likes. All you have to do is make sure you hear and pick up the phone. If you don't hear the phone, don't worry. Providing he's interested he'll try again.

Option two: make him work for your number

Let's look again at the same conversation. This time you can playfully tease him until he asks for your number.

He says:
"Hey, I saw your profile and noticed you like skydiving. Me too! Fancy a skydive together?"

You respond:
"Hey, sounds fun! Amy"

He says:
"Sure, how about next week? We could have a chat on the phone if you'd like?"

You say:
"Sounds great, but you haven't asked for my number yet! Just saying..."

He says:
"Silly me, please can I have your number? I'd love to call you sometime."

You say:
"Well, since you asked so nicely! It's 07659 867143."
If he asks for your number, give it to him.

Option three: The Chivalry Line

This is my own invention, and is a playful way to exchange numbers. If you want to play it safe, then use the approach as described in option one or two.

However, if you want to be a little adventurous give him 'The Chivalry Line.' This is how it works. I'm going to share part of the email exchange between my husband and me, to show how he got my number.

He wrote:
"Hi, I hope all is well with you and you had a good day. Photo attached as promised.
Take care."

I responded:
"Ok great. Thanks for forwarding."

He wrote:
"Hi, nice to hear from you. Where are you from? If you fancy a chat my mobile number is 07654 123 543"

I responded:
"Hey, thanks for your number. Isn't it chivalrous for the guy to call the girl? Just saying."

He wrote:
"Nice to hear from you. I am all for chivalry but I do not have your number! How is your day going? Look forward to chatting soon."

I responded:
"Well then, I don't recall you asking for my number. Should you ask, then maybe, just maybe, I'll oblige."

He wrote:
"Good evening. I hope you had a good weekend. I would be honoured and delighted if you would forward your number. And we may chat sometime soon... :-) Look forward to getting to know you better. Take care."

I responded:
"Well, since you asked so nicely. My moby is 07654 123 543."

He wrote:
"Thank you for your number, you are most kind. Look forward to speaking soon."

2

What to Do If He Has Your Number and Doesn't Call Straight Away

Don't panic! He has your number. He calls when he calls.

Does that mean he's not into me?
No. Not at all.
Sometimes men don't call immediately. Mainly because he wants to have enough time available for a proper conversation. He might be busy preparing for an important pitch. His sister may have recently given birth, or he might be planning a surprise 80th birthday party for his grandma!
Who knows?
It could take him two weeks to call. Remember, when he does call, always be polite.

Don't say:
"Jeez, you took your time."
Be pleasant, nice, and don't say anything negative. Also, if you've been hopping around the room waiting for his call or wondering why he hasn't called – you're not busy enough.

3

What to Do If He Asks for Your Number on Chat or Instant Messenger

Here's a typical conversation and here's how to navigate:

Him:
"Hey"

Response:
"Hi"

Him:
"How are you?"

Response:
"Good thanks."

Him:
"I'm in a rush. Can I have your number? I can call you now."

Response:
Either log off OR give him your number and log off.
You can say:
"Sure, I'm on 07896 123 543"
Or give him your dating email address

Why do men do this?

Easy: chat is quick and simple. If he knows you're available via instant messaging, then this is exactly what he'll do. Yes, you can respond to chat and instant message when **you** want to — but that doesn't mean you're always 'on.' And don't worry, if he wants to date you; he can always ask again.

4

How to Move the Conversation on from Email to Phone

You don't move the conversation on, and you don't suggest he calls you.

For example, you don't say:
"Call me on the number I gave."

Remember *The Rules:* the man leads. It's up to him to move the conversation on. Either he calls or he doesn't. If he texts and asks for a date, that's OK. You can accept the date via text.

If you're online dating and he doesn't ask for your number after seven emails, he's a NEXT.

If he continues to email, and doesn't ask for your number or suggests a date, ignore his emails. Read them if you want, but there's no need to reply.

Providing he has your number, rest assured that any man who wants to date you, will get in touch. And they normally do.

Some men will text once they have your number. They sometimes do this to verify that your number is real. The extremely keen types call straight away. And who can blame them! You are a creature unlike any other.

If he calls, you can answer. Make sure you're the one who ends the call — after around 10 minutes. If you met online and this is the first time you're talking, you can end the first call after 15-20 minutes. The point here is not to spend hours on the phone.

Sometimes when a new suitor calls for the very first time, it can be difficult to end the call after ten minutes. Judge the conversation and don't reveal too much at this very early stage.

5

How to Move the Conversation on from Text to Calls

When you start dating, men will text you. Keep in mind that all texts are not equal. Neither do you need to reply to every text.

Men won't lose interest because you missed a text here or there. Men are problem solvers. When he can't get you via text, he'll call. (Yes, he'll work this out all by himself).

The simplest and easiest way to move the conversation on from text to phone, is to ignore any texts that don't require a response.

In the early dating stages and prior to meeting face to face, simply ignore any non-date related texts. In another words, if he's not trying to date you, forget about him.

6

How to Reply to Common Texts or Emails

Here's what I mean about messages which don't need a response:

- *"Hey, how are you?"*
- *"Hey beautiful how's your day going?"*
- *"What are you doing today?"*

Delete these texts from your phone and pretend they never existed.

If he asks:
"Hey, did you get my text?"

You can say:
"Hey, so sorry, you wouldn't believe how bad I am with texting. My brother is a huge texter and my lack of texting drives him insane."

Or you can say:
"Hey so sorry. I'm not a great texter."

I have to emphasise there's no need to panic. The world doesn't end. Men don't stop chasing because you don't text back.

What happens instead, is that he calls.

Remember, when moving the conversation on, you can't tell him what to do. It's better to train him via actions. What this means, is not responding to every single text immediately and instantaneously. On that note, if he calls, try your best to take his call. Don't ignore his calls on purpose. Since, he now knows you're responsive to calls, he'll start calling you.

He texts:
"Hi, this is Neil from the site."

You respond:
Ignore.
Wait for him to ask you out or call. These types of texts don't require a response.

Why do men do this?
If you're online dating, you'll quickly get used to receiving these types of messages. Once you've swapped numbers, some men send a type of 'checking in' text. Let him, rest assured there is no need to reply. Again, his phone is in his hand, he can always call you.

He emails or texts:
"Hey, give me a call or text on the number I gave you."

You respond:
Since he already has your number, ignore this text and wait for him to call. There's no need to respond.

Why do men do this?
He thinks he's being helpful. He doesn't realise you don't call men and that he has to call first. Teach him with your actions. And, don't worry; if he's interested he will call.

He emails:
"You look good."

You respond:

There's no need to respond to one word or one liner emails. You can safely ignore and delete these types of message.

Why do men do this?

Online dating is tough. Let's give them a point for trying though.

He says:

"Let me know when you're free?"

You respond:

If he texts the above, wait between four and twenty four hours. Respond back with
"Sure, will do" — and then ignore.

Why do men do this?

Again, he's being polite and considerate. He's trying to save time. He's thinking *"if she tells me when she's free, I have more chance of catching her."* Men are smart!

He texts or emails via an online dating site:

"Hi, how are you?"

You respond:

If you're dating, especially online dating, you'll get many one liner texts and emails. You can safely ignore all one line messages.

Why do men do this?

They've sent you a blanket email. It's a little like spam. They've probably emailed the same one liner to lots and lots of other girls. Don't bother replying. Only reply to men who have taken the time to read and mention something in your written profile.

If you're dating and once you've swapped numbers, some men will send the above as an 'ice breaker text'.

Sometimes men are simply bored, they're either standing in a queue, stuck in a dull meeting or are undertaking some similar mind-numbing task. Basically, they're just passing time. You are worth more than this. Let him 'pass time,' as long as it's not your time.

7

How to Get Him to Call at a Time Convenient for You

You can't!

That said, you can ensure he doesn't call at crazy hours.

The majority of men are sensible, and men who want to impress you, wouldn't dream of giving you a booty call or calling at unsociable hours.

That being said, some men will call late. For the most part they're not doing it on purpose.

Buy yourself a dating phone. Turn it off at 9.30pm or whatever time feels appropriate for you. Switch your dating phone back on again in the morning. He'll soon realise that you're unavailable after 9.30pm.

If he calls late you can either:

- Not respond.
- Pick up and say: *"Oh hey, thanks for the call, it's really late. How about we chat tomorrow?"*

If he called late, don't feel obliged to stay on the phone. It's up to you to set the boundaries and 'teach' him how to treat you.

8

How to Guide Him to Ask for Your Number in Person

Exchanging numbers is much easier in person. If you meet someone when you're out and he asks for your number; give it to him. Don't play games and don't reject him because you want to 'test' whether he really likes you or not. Providing you like him, if he asks, give your number.

Don't offer your number out though. He has to ask!

But what if he's really cute?

No exceptions! He must ask you.

Should you type your number into his phone?

No! The phone stays in his hands. Let him type your number in.

What if he asks you to give him a missed call?

A lot of men like this approach. Don't let him get away with it! Make an excuse.

Tell him: *"Ohh sorry, my phone is all the way at the bottom of my bag."*

What if he asks you to send a text to confirm your number?

He's being lazy! Resist again. Use the same excuse, or tell him you're out of battery.

Don't make it into a big deal. Either he wants your number or he doesn't.

Another solution is to try going out without your phone. If

you try this approach, make sure you've pre-booked a cab home. If you're out, you can always borrow a friend's phone in case of an emergency.

9

What If He Asks for Your Number But You're Not Interested?

Do your bit for humanity, and give him your number.

Go on, make his day; give him your dating phone number. You don't have to take his call, but at least it'll boost his ego.

Otherwise thank him. Make an excuse; maybe tell him you already have a boyfriend. Be gentle. Remember, what goes around comes around.

10

Why Do Men Ask Personal Questions Straight Away?

Sometimes men will ask personal questions, for example:

- *"What do you do for a living?"*
- *"Where do you live?"*
- *"Do you drive?"*

These are typical dating style questions. And, if he asks, answer the questions honestly yet mysteriously. Go ahead and tell him what you do. Tell him the part of town you live in, but don't disclose your full address. In regards to driving, tell him whether you do or don't drive. He doesn't need to know what make of car you have yet.

Why do men ask this straight away?
None of these are trick questions. And there's no point getting yourself into a flap either.

He's trying to get to know you. He's asking questions in order to build a picture of you. How else is he supposed to get to know you?

Have you been feeling stuck in this area? If you need more help with this dating question, get my free video and other great resources at indiakang.com/resources.

11

What to Do If He Ends the Message with 'x' in the Form of a Kiss

Nothing.

There's no need to reciprocate.

Even if he signs off with an X, it doesn't oblige you to do the same.

Most men will start to add an X, as early as the first or second text. At this stage the X means nothing at all. Try not to read anything into it. Remember: when a man is talking, you watch his actions and ignore his words. There's little point in adding an X and saying how gorgeous you are, if he isn't trying to date you.

The times for you to add an X in the form of a kiss are few and far between. If you're ever in doubt, leave it out.

When can I start to add an X?

Once you're very happily exclusive. And even then, use them sparingly. Once you're married, you can add as many as you like and as often as you want.

12

How to End the Call First

Here are three ways to end the call first:

- *"Well, thanks for calling, but I'd better go."*
- *"It was great chatting, but I have to go... have a nice day/evening."*
- *"Great chatting, but I'd better go."*

13

How to Manage Questions About Facebook

There are so many ways to manage this scenario.

If you do decide to accept his Facebook request, be sure to keep your status updates to a minimum. Another good preventive measure is to clean up your Facebook page beforehand. Remove and/or delete any unsuitable status updates and pictures, much like you would for potential employers.

If he sends you a Facebook request, you have the following choices:

- Don't accept his Facebook request. Not for everyone but very possible to do. I did.
- Accept, and put him on a limited view. You can manage this via Facebook's privacy settings.
- Blocking him on Facebook will prevent him from ever finding you. A little draconian but it's one less social media channel to worry about. If he can't find you, he can't add you. If he asks, you can say: *"Oh really, you can't find me? Yeah, I don't really use Facebook much."*

He says or texts:
"Hey, I sent you a Facebook friend request."

You respond:
"Oh, did you? Ok I'll take a look. Sorry, I don't really use Facebook much."

Or
"OK, I'll take a look later." And then forget about it.

He asks:
"Are you on Facebook?"

You respond:
You can either say:
"Yes, but I don't really use it much."
Or you can say:
"Yes, my Facebook name is India Kang."

It's entirely up to you which approach you take. Yes, you can accept his Facebook request. You don't need to accept straight away. Once you accept, put him on limited view. If he has full access to your Facebook, ensure not to continually post status updates. Above all else, make sure you stay off his wall.

14

How to Keep Your Privacy While Dating

You may not want him to find you on Facebook or to Google you.

In this instance, set your Facebook privacy settings to high so he can't find you. Google yourself too. This way you know what he'll see and you can prepare for it. It never hurts to be prepared.

Unless you've got something to hide, you should be safe. Remember to use your dating phone. Don't reveal your home address too soon. And delete anything on Facebook that you don't want him to see.

What if he asks my surname?

It all depends on how comfortable you are with disclosing your surname and your culture. In some cultures, it's imperative to disclose your surname. In these cultures, sharing the same surname means you can't marry. You share the same lineage which is seen as incestuous.

If this is your culture, and he asks, tell him. If you share the same surname, you can't date anyway.

If you live in a culture where this isn't so important, there are three choices.

Simply tell him, or playfully say any of the following:

"Well, that's classified information." (giggle giggle)
"My Dad says, I'm not allowed to share personal information with people I don't know! What's a girl to do? I have to respect his wishes."

"I couldn't say. At least not yet."

If he asks for your surname, you can certainly ask him to disclose the same information.

How do I find out his surname?
We met online and I don't know!
Look for clues in his email address, profile name etc. Other than that, you don't ask him! You wait for him to tell you.

What you mean I can't ask?
What's the rush? You'll find out soon enough.

Case Study

There's one guy I really liked on a dating site. A couple of months ago, we exchanged numbers and texted back and forth but there was never any mention of a date.

Recently I updated my profile and added some new pictures. All of a sudden he messaged and asked me out for lunch. I hastily agreed, and then he asked me what my name was! Should I tell him we've already spoken, or should I act like I don't remember him?

Response:

If you're online dating, this will happen. Men will email, forget they emailed, and email again. You'll probably even receive exactly the same message as well. They're not morons, they're basically sitting at their computers blasting out cut and paste messages to see who bites. This is why you don't read too much into generic cut and paste emails. Only respond to emails where he has taken the time to mention personal information about your profile.

Here's an example.

If, in your profile, you wrote you love swimming and he writes:
"Great profile, I love swimming too! I'm actually training for a swimathon at the moment."
In this instance you can respond.

However, if he writes:
"Hey, great pics and great profile, would love to get to know you better."
You can safely ignore this message.

If a guy doesn't remember he previously wrote to you, then you don't remember either. He already forgot you once; don't be upset if he forgets again.

Men who want to date you, don't forget you. These men dream, think about and imagine you!

PART TWO

QUESTIONS ASKED DURING THE DATING PROCESS

1

How to Respond to Common Texts and Emails

Dating is very much a process. If you're new to dating, you'll soon realise that men love to text. Keep in mind, that it's best to start as you mean to go on. What I mean, is, that once you start engaging with his texts, it's harder to reverse engineer.

Only respond to texts that are related to date planning. The majority of other texts will fall into the 'do not respond' category.

Here are some examples. If he texts:
"Hi, how are you?"
"Wanna hook up?"
Or
Any one – or two-word texts. For example:

- *"Hey beautiful"*
- *"How's your day going?"*
- *"Got any interesting plans for this evening?"*
- *"What are you up to?"*
- *"I dreamt about you last night, wanna hear about it?"*
- *"There's a two for one offer on sushi this evening. I have a discount voucher, wanna come?"*

Your response:
IGNORE.

No need to reply. Delete the text and pretend you never received it.

Why some men do this?
They're bored! Don't worry, I'm sure he'll find something else to keep him occupied.

He texts:
"Hi, I just tried to reach you. Call me when you get this text."

You respond:
If you met via an online dating site and swapped phone numbers, you'll find some men will send a preliminary text message as above.

Yes, you can respond to this message. Be warned that if you do (especially at this very early dating stage) he'll know you're available on text, which means he'll continue to text.

You have two options:

- Ignore the text and wait for him to call or to ask for a date. If you ignore the text nothing bad will happen. What usually happens is that, he'll call.
- Or you can respond with *"Great thanks, speak soon."*

Why do men do this?
Yes, many men will do this. It's his way of 'checking in' with you. They're not bad people; as humans we're all wired to find the easiest solution to a problem. He thinks by sending a quick text, you'll acknowledge his text and respond.

2

"Is Now a Good Time to Talk?"

If he calls and asks the above question. You can say any of the following:

"Yes"

Or

"Perfect timing, I've literally just walked in."

Only use the second response if you've missed a few of his calls. Saying this will make him feel very successful.

Wow! He's managed to pin you down on the phone. What a massive achievement. Is he a superhero or what!

3

He Texts: "Looking Forward to Seeing You Tomorrow"

If he contacts you before the date with the above message, you don't need to respond back. Of course, he's looking forward to seeing you. You're hot stuff.

What if he thinks I'm not interested?

Men don't think like women. Quite the opposite. And, if anything it will only increase his interest levels. Men love a challenge and a chase. They also love hard to get, easy to be with girls.

Case Study

I met a guy online. We had a great couple of dates. For our second date, we went to an amusement arcade, which was great fun. After the date, he gave me a hug, and tried to kiss me. When I got home he texted to say 'what a great time' he had, and how I was more beautiful in person.

Does this mean he is really into me?

Response:

Men who are into you ask for dates. If he asks for another date, then yes, he likes you. If he doesn't ask, then he's just not that into you.

His sweet text means nothing either. Watch his actions, ignore his words.

As long as he's asking you for dates, booking in advance, paying and travelling to you, then yes, you can assume he likes you.

If you found this case study useful, I have more case studies available at indiakang.com/resources

4

He Says: "Let Me Know a Good Time to Call?"

You respond:
"Hey, anytime is great. Speak soon!"

He may text/email/instant message:
"OK I'll try you later."

You can either ignore or you can respond with:
"OK sounds great."

After this short exchange, wait for him to call. Remember — he calls when he calls.

Why do men do this?

This is another very common text message. You will get asked this heaps so don't fight it. Use the responses in this guide, embrace it and go with it.

In case you're thinking:

"I'm really busy. I have a small child. In the evenings, I'm with my son or at Pilates; I lead a very busy life. Why can't I tell him a time to call?"

You can if you really want to, unfortunately that doesn't mean he'll call at that specific time. And remember, we don't tell men what to do!

If you did give him a time, for example if you said:

"Hey, I'm free between 7pm and 9pm."

This leaves him with a very small window in which to call. Give him the freedom to call when he calls. If he misses you, it doesn't matter, he can always try you again.

5

He Asks: "How Come You Don't Text?"

If you're dating and practicing *The Rules*, this will make you stand out from all the other girls.

Some men will initially find your behaviour bizarre, mainly because the majority of girls text back straight away. Don't be shocked if he has a perplexed look on his face.

If he asks the above question, you can respond with either:

"I know, I know, my family say the same thing. I'm not a great texter, never have been."
Or
"Don't I? So sorry, I guess I've been a little busy, I promise to try harder."
Or
"You know what, I started texting you back but I got distracted, so sorry."

Try and act a little surprised, pretend like you really didn't realise that you don't text much. Remember to smile too.

If you're following *The Rules*, you won't be replying straight away, neither will you accept last minute dates, which make all the above lines very convincing. Keep your actions consistent with your words and therefore believable.

Why do men ask this question?
Men are often perplexed when they meet a girl who doesn't

immediately respond to texts. Everyone is constantly checking his or her phone. Most girls text men back in nanoseconds!

You don't, which makes you different to the other girls. This is great, as you're the one who will stick in his mind.

Case Study

If I'm on a Date and He Asks If I'm Seeing Anyone Else.

Do I tell him yes or no?

If I say, *"Yes, I am,"* he might think I'm sleeping around.

On the other hand, if I say, *"No, I'm not,"* he might think I'm not sought after enough.

I'm confused. What should I do?

Response:

I'm going to give you a little analogy. This scenario is a little like going for an interview and the interviewer asks:

"Are you interviewing anywhere else?"

Or

"Are you waiting to hear back from any other jobs?"

If you say:

"No, this is the only job I've interviewed for."

They'll think:

"She can't be that good, maybe we shouldn't hire her. The fact that no one else wants to interview her, may mean she's no good."

If you say:

"Yes, I've been interviewing for months and months."

They'll think:
"She's had so many interviews yet no one wants to hire her. I wonder why? Maybe there's something wrong with her."

Instead you say something vague like:
"Well I have a few irons in the fire."

You haven't said yes or no.
It's the same for dating.
If he asks, if you're seeing anyone else, playfully say:
"Well then... that would be telling." And then laugh.

Remember to keep the mystery! He can make up his own conclusions; you don't need to spell it out. The less you say the better.

If he wants to ensure you only date him, he can always ask for exclusivity. Until then, you're both free to date whomever you want.

6

He Asks: "What's with the Two Word Text Responses?"

You have two options;
Either ignore his text or respond with: *"I guess I'm not much of a texter"* or use any of the aforementioned responses.

Why men ask this:
Most girls respond to messages within nanoseconds. You don't, which is a little odd for him. Cut him some slack, he's not used to dating a *Rules* girl.

7

He Asks: "Are You on Skype? We Could Skype?"

You respond:
"No, I don't really use Skype very much."

Tone:
Be matter of fact.

Why men ask this?

If he can 'meet' you on Skype, he will. This doesn't mean you can't Skype. If you're in a long distance relationship, you may have a Skype date in between his visits. By long distance, I mean where you live in different countries.

If you're not in a long distance relationship, let's say, you've had a couple of dates and he wants to Skype in between dates, don't bother. He can see you on the date. Skype shouldn't become a substitute for real face-to-face dates.

8

He Asks: "Do You IM or WhatsApp?"

You respond:
"Yes, but I don't use it much"

He may say:
"What really? Why not? Everyone is on chat these days?"
You can playfully say
"If I was on WhatsApp, I wouldn't get anything done. And, I don't think my boss would be happy!"

Note:
If you're on IM or have WhatsApp and are serious about dating, you may want to consider deleting the app and staying off chat for a short time.

"What?!? Are you crazy? All my friends and family are on WhatsApp!" I hear you say.

If you can muster the self-discipline not to constantly check your messages, then OK.

Be smart–don't let an app get in the way of finding Mr. Right. You can always reinstall the app at a later stage. It's not like it's gone forever!

In the meantime, you can stay connected with family and friends via email, Skype, Facebook, Twitter, LinkedIn, Instagram, phone etc. There are many alternatives. Please give my suggestions some thought. I'm not saying you should avoid technology. Rather, I'm offering a short-term solution in order to lose the battle and win the war. Deleting the app is one less platform to worry about and will 'force' him to either text or call instead.

9

"What Are Your Plans for the Weekend?"

When men ask this question, there's often no need to respond. If he messages on a Friday or Saturday morning, ignore the message. If he messages on a Wednesday or before, you can say: *"Nothing concrete yet."*

Your response depends on how long you've been dating. If he's a new guy, there's no need to respond.

Alternatively, you can say:
"You know; the usual."
He may ask for an explanation: *"Like what?"*
Keep it vague and say *"you know; this and that."*

If you're on a date and he asks, again you can respond with:
"This and that." Remember to smile too.
If he's insistent, and won't accept "this and that" as a response, then you could say:
"Well I'm meeting the girls for lunch and we're thinking about going to a party."
Try your best to be vague.
Unless he's asking for a date, your weekend plans are none of his business.

10

He Says: "I See You're Divorced or Separated"

You respond:
"Yes"

He may ask:
"What happened?"

You respond:
"Not much"
 Or
"We weren't compatible".

Tone:
Answer this question nonchalantly, like it was no big deal. Do not under any circumstance character assassinate your ex; even if he was the worst guy in the whole wide world. Keep it to yourself.

Why men ask this?
For some men and in some cultures, divorce is a big stigma. If it helps you feel better, I'm divorced and it never stopped me dating. Yes, some men don't want to date a divorcee; don't let that bother you. There are plenty of others who will! Don't be ashamed of your divorce. It's life.

Men WILL ask you about your divorce. In my culture, they ask in hushed tones almost as if it's a crime! It's no crime. You're divorced, life goes on. Answer his questions with a simple YES or a NO and that's it. After that change the subject. Don't feel obliged to divulge any details. Again, it's none of his business.

To help you further, take comfort in the fact that many people remarry after a divorce.

11

He Asks: "Have You Dated Much?"

You respond:
"Emmm face-to-face dates no, not that many. How about you?"
  Or
"No not really, I've only just started dating."
  Or
"That would be telling." And then smile.

Tone:
Act quizzical and puzzled, *of course you haven't dated much.* You're a creature unlike any other. Any guy would be lucky to have you, and only rare gems get to date you.

Don't bad mouth any of your dates EVER. Even if you've had a zillion bad dates, you've been dating for the past seven years, fed up and never want to date again, zip the lip. He doesn't need to know. Dating isn't therapy.

Have you been feeling stuck in this area? If you need more help with this dating question, get my free video and other great resources at indiakang.com/resources.

12

He Asks: "Are You Dating Anyone Else?"

You can respond with either:
"That would be telling. I couldn't possibly say." And then laugh.
Or
"Emm, well... I get out."
Or if you're feeling playful, you can laugh and say:
"That's top secret, I'd love to tell you, if only I could!"

Tone:
Cheeky and very playful.

Why do men ask this question?
Sometimes men want to gauge the competition, it's nothing sinister and no, they're not being control freaks. Often when a man finds his dream girl, he wants her off the dating scene quick. Asking this question helps him to get a 'feel' for things.

The worst thing you can say is:
"Yeah, I've dated heaps and heaps."
Even if this is true, there's no need to tell him. Maintaining an air of mystery will win you brownie points.

Other forms of this question include:
"Are you talking to anyone else?"
"Do you date a lot?"

13

He Asks: "Are You Even Interested in Me?"

You can either say:
"Well, I certainly wouldn't waste your time."
Or
"I'm enjoying getting to know you.'

Why do men ask this?
Once again, they're confused and have no idea where they stand with you. You agree to dates, turn up and are friendly, yet in between dates you disappear.

It's normal for him to feel a little on edge. He's looking for reassurance. Give him a little, just a little mind you. Responding in the above way, will keep him motivated to carry on wooing you.

14

"What Are You Looking for in a Man?"

This is a very common question. All men ask this question; here are a couple of creative responses:

"Emmm, what am I looking for?" Pause – *"I've never really thought about it."*

Or

"I'll let you know once I've found him!" And then giggle.

Tone of voice:
Be cheery, but thoughtful.

Why do all men ask the same questions?
Urban dating is tough and everyone is trying the best they can. No one really knows the correct *modus operandi*. Dating is similar to looking for a job, and having to answer the same interview questions over and over again. Dating works in exactly the same way.

15

He Asks: "What's Your Ideal Man?"

You respond:
"Emmm... I'm not sure; I'd have to think about that."

Tone:
Again playful.

Why do men ask this?
They want to know if they have a shot with you. That said, there's no need to answer this question in any detail.

For example, if you said your ideal man is Brad Pitt and he looks nothing like Brad Pitt, he may assume he has no chance with you and he'll feel deflated.

Of course, you know exactly what you're looking for. And you know who your ideal man is too, just keep it yourself, at least for now. He may not tick all your boxes, give him a chance. What's the worst that can happen?

Don't give him a laundry list either. Don't say *"well, I want someone who is strong yet gentle, masculine yet in touch with his feminine side; a go getter who is equally happy to spend time watching a DVD."*

Presenting a laundry list may work against you. He'll walk away thinking, *"Goodness, she certainly wants a lot! I'm not sure I'm up to the job."*

What if you asked him the same question and he said:
"Well, I really think Selena Gomez is HOT. She's so hot. She's my ideal woman."

Let's say you look nothing like Selena Gomez. How great would you feel?

16

He Asks: "What Time Do You Finish Work?"

The answers to this question depend on two factors:

1. The timing of the text.
2. Where you are in the dating journey.

If you're at the very beginning and there's no confirmed date in the diary, you can ignore this text. It's a pointless text. It's none of his business what time you finish work. You barely know him.

If you have a confirmed date in the diary and he asks the above, you can also ignore it.

Why?
There's no need to respond. You have a date in the diary at 7pm. As long as you get to the date in time, your schedule is none of his business. If you're exclusive and have been dating seriously for months, you can answer, although chances are at this stage, he'll already know your schedule.

Why do men ask this question?
No more than chit chat. Don't give it your precious headspace. Get back to work and make sure to turn up to your date on time.

17

"Fancy a Hook Up?"

Ignore!

Ignore any of these types of messages. The only response is to delete his details from your contact list.

Any guy who asks for a 'hook up' is a NEXT!

18

He Asks: "Do You Have Any Dating Stories?"

You respond:
"No, not really. I guess I've been really lucky!"

Tone:
Be matter of fact. Even if you've had thousands of bad dates, don't tell him. Simply use the response above and deflect the question. It's not in your interests to share any dating horror stories. He can share all he wants, you must hold back. The less you say the better.

Why?
He doesn't need to know how much you've dated. Don't sit there and bemoan dating. Everyone else, and all the other girls, are doing exactly that. Be different. Trust me, he'll notice.

Why do men ask this question?
It's no different to an interviewer asking *"tell me about your past jobs?"* Even if you hated your last job and your boss was a moron, you'd never verbalise this. Dating is no different.

Other derivatives of this type of question include the following:

- *"Have you dated much?"*
- *"How come you don't have any dating stories?"*

In both these instances, respond in the same way.

19

He Says: "Tell Me About Yourself?"

You respond:
"Sure, what would you like to know?"

He may say:
"I don't know, tell me something about you?"

You can respond with:
"Well my name is Abbey, I'm 5ft 8 and I make the best banana cake. So how about you?"

Tone:
Light hearted and playful.

Why do men ask this question?

This is a standard dating question. He wants to get to know you better. Again, it's no different to an interviewer asking: *"Tell me more about you?"*

Of course you are selective in what you choose to reveal. And, you don't talk on and on. Remember to ask the question back, you'll be surprised how much men love to talk about themselves. Let him. It's a great opportunity to listen and take notes.

20

He Says: "Tell Me Three Things About Yourself?"

You respond in the same way:
"Sure, what would you like to know?"

He may say:
"Emmm... I don't know. Tell me about you?"

You can say:
"Ok, here are three things, my name is Ruth, I'm 5ft 6 and I like running. How about you?"

Tone:
Be cheerful, and direct the question back to him.

Why do men ask this?
Again, he's trying to get to know you better. That said, don't be tempted to divulge too much personal information. If you end up having a relationship or getting married, there's the rest of your lives to get to know each other better!

21

He Asks: "How Long Have You Been Single?"

Depending on your circumstances, you can respond in any of the following ways:

- *"A couple of years."*
- *"About a year."*
- *"Emmm... a while."*

Again, don't talk about any of your past relationships. And don't say any of the following:

- *"I've been single for years and years and can't seem to find anyone."*
- *"My last boyfriend was a jerk and I hate all men."*
- *"I'm so bored with dating. All men are weird."*
- *"I'm still getting over my last relationship."*

I could go on and on about what not to say. Hopefully you get the idea. Keep your answers vague; less is always more.

22

He Asks "How Do You Find This Whole Dating Scene?"

You respond:
"Good, thank you. I think I've been lucky."

Tone:
Be happy and positive. Bad things never happen to you. Act if necessary.

23

He Asks: "Is There Anywhere You'd Like to Go?"

You respond:
"Emmm don't mind. What do you think?"

Tone:
Be indecisive. *'Emmm'* a little. And, then pause for him to work it out.

Why do men ask this question?
They're trying to please you. They want to do the best they can. They are also feeling their way around dating.

Believe it or not, men want to make you happy. When he succeeds at making you happy, he releases testosterone which makes him happy. Which means, he will want to do more things to make you happy.

Men will do anything to put a smile on your face. Let him lead and follow. Don't forget to show gratitude! Whatever he suggests as the date plan is fine by you. Go with it!

Of course, if he suggests something distasteful, feel free to end the date, go home and delete his number.

24

"Are You Still Ok for Tonight?"

You respond:
"Yes. See you there."
(Only respond if there's a scheduled date in the diary.)

Why do men do this?

It's very common for men to text on the day to confirm plans. Some men (and may I add very few) will confirm in advance.

If you have a date scheduled at 6pm, he may confirm at 3pm. The 'better' ones may text and confirm in the morning. Either way, don't panic!

Don't be tempted to text him to ask about date plans. You have to wait for him to contact you. He will. Go about your business and don't think too much about the date. It's only a date!

Get ready as if the dating is happening, and make sure to have a backup plan. The backup plan may simply be to go home, drink wine and watch TV. If you can, go to a speed-dating or singles event. Dial a friend and go out for drinks or dinner. If you're all dressed up with nowhere to go – maybe go out for dinner by yourself. What's the worst that could happen?

If you're uncomfortable with any of these suggestions, maybe sit in a coffee shop and read your book. At the very least walk home some of the way. Take comfort that while walking home, some men may see you.

I'm not saying men will jump out of their cars and ask for your number. It's more trying to make the best out of the situation.

25

"What's the Plan for Tonight?"

You respond:
"Hey, whatever you pick is fine."
Or
"I'm happy with whatever you pick."

Why do men do this?
The odd guy will send this type of message, although for the most part you'll already have an agreed meeting place.

He's asking because he thinks he's being polite by handing you the reins. He hasn't met you yet and probably wants to impress you. It would be awful if he picked a venue or cuisine that you hated. Wouldn't that be a bad way to impress your dream girl?

Let's say he's from out of town and doesn't know your area, which is a highly probable scenario. Let's also assume, you met online or via an app, and you don't want him to know where you live. In this instance, to avoid the back and forth texting, the best thing to do is pick a landmark near you. A tube stop or some other landmark is normally a good choice.

Here's a sample conversation:
Him: *"I don't know your area, where should we meet?"*
You: *"I don't mind, what do you think about outside Piccadilly tube station?"*
Him: *"OK, what time can you meet?"*
You: *"Any time after 7pm works this end."*

Him: *"OK, how about 7.30pm and we can find somewhere for drinks nearby."*
You: *"Sounds great, see you then."*

Responding back in this way means he gets to lead, you're not telling him what to do and you're being light and breezy.

26

"Hey, I'm Thinking of Going to a Movie, Any Interest?"

If he's asking for a last minute date, you can respond back with:
"Sounds great! It's a shame I already have plans."

Don't worry. If he's interested, he'll soon start asking days in advance.

If he's giving you advance warning, you can respond with:
"Sure, sounds great."

27

He Asks: "Are You Free Tonight?"

You respond:
There's no need to reply to this message. The best option is to ignore completely. If you really want to, you can wait 24 hours and respond with:

"Hey, just seen your text, sorry. Hope you're good?"

Why do men do this?
He's asking for a last-minute date, and we don't accept last-minute dates. Maybe his other date bailed and he's at a loose end. Maybe he's had a really hard day at work and fancies some company to help him unwind. Maybe he's just bored. The worst thing you can do is accept. Accepting a last-minute date sets a precedent. And you're not a last minute girl.

28

"Are You Willing to Relocate?"

This is an important question which is best answered honestly.

If you're not willing to relocate. I would encourage you to focus your search locally.

If you're adamant about never relocating, you can answer by saying:

"No, I don't want to move. I really love where I live."

Even then, who knows what the future holds. He may have to relocate for a new job or a family matter.

Alternatively you can say:

"I'm not completely against moving. I guess for the right person it's something I'd consider."

Why do men ask this?

He wants to know whether you're open and willingly to relocate. If you're not, he may not bother dating you. Generally, men want an easy life. He wants to know early on if 'relocating' is likely to cause problems further down the line.

If he wants to relocate and you won't, he'll look for someone who isn't going to hold him back. Men really want an easy life!

29

How to Respond to Cutesy Messages

In the beginning of the relationship he may text any of the following messages:

- *"I really miss spending time with you. We have so much in common."*
- *"Good morning, beautiful."*
- *"I'm cooking dinner, and was thinking of you."*

None of these messages require a response, here are your two options:

- Delete and don't reply
- Send back a smiley face and nothing else

"His message is so sincere and nice," I hear you say.

Here's the difference, if he'd said:
"Hey beautiful, great meeting you, when are you free?"
In this instance, you can respond because he's asking you out. Confused?
Don't be! Remember, any man who wants to date you, will pin you down. Men don't lose interest because you didn't respond back to his messages.

30

Why Do Men Send Random Messages and What Do They Mean?

Men often send meaningless messages, for a number of reasons:

- They're bored.
- They have some spare time, no plans, and thought they'd try their luck at getting you out.
- They're standing in a queue and thought they'd pass some time.
- They're stuck in a boring meeting and need some distraction.

What should you do?
Delete the text and pretend it never came.

What does it mean?
Not much. Don't over analyse. Men who want to date you, will take you out. They don't play games and they don't keep you hanging. They also want you off the dating scene. They don't want to lose you to a less deserving competitor.

31

He Called, We Had a Great Chat, and He Didn't Ask Me Out. What Do I Do?

Don't worry. He can always call again — and normally he will. If he continues to call, yet doesn't ask for a date, stop taking his calls. We want dates, not pointless calls.

32

A Guy I Met Online Has Called Five Times. I Keep Missing His Calls. Should I Text Him Back?

Here's how to navigate.

You can say:
"Hey sorry, crazy busy at work, speak soon."
Alternatively wait for him to call again.

Chances are, if, he's already called five times, he'll call again. Please have your phone somewhere you can hear it. Make sure your intentions are correct and don't miss his calls on purpose. It's not a game.

33

What to Do If He Texts and Calls, Yet Never Arranges Date Plans

He's not into you.

He likes chatting to you. He might even *Bookmark* you for when times are lean.

That's about it. Don't respond. Ignore his texts and calls.

You don't need to say anything to him either. Your silence and lack of response is more than enough.

Case Study

I'm talking to this guy online. He lives a couple of hours away. I guess it could be a potential long-distance relationship.

My first response to his email was short and sweet.

"Thank you. You seem interesting."

Since exchanging numbers he's texted every day. We've exchanged over a dozen text exchanges. The closest he got to organising a date, was to ask whether we should ride our bikes together. I responded by saying:

"Sounds great."

He is yet to follow up on the bicycle date. Instead, he wrote a text asking what I find interesting about him.

Should I stop responding to him?

Response:

Yes, absolutely stop responding to his texts. This guy is a time waster. Men who want to date you, don't hang around, mainly because they don't want to lose you. They want you *off* the dating scene.

It's a little like that designer dress you want. You've seen it in the shop window and now it's reduced. Do you wait a few days to think about it, or, do you stand outside the shop before it even opens? I'm guessing the latter, right? You want to get there first before anyone else does. The dress is yours and yours alone and you're going to beat off the competition!

Men think in the same way. They don't pointlessly text and text.

You can help yourself and stop responding to his texts. When you stop responding to his texts, either he'll call or disappear.

Finally, two hours is not a long-distance relationship. Men will happily travel hours for their favourite sports team. Two hours is nothing. If he wants you, he will happily travel two hours and more.

Case Study

I met this guy online a few months ago. We haven't managed to meet yet, mainly because we both went on long trips aboard. He recently returned and finally suggested we meet for a drink.

He wrote *"I am free tomorrow, do you still fancy that drink?"*

What do I do?

Response:

Politely turn him down because we don't accept last-minute dates. Tell him *"Sounds great, shame I already have plans for tomorrow."*

If he's interested, he'll try to arrange for another day, otherwise he'll disappear.

Either way it's a win.

If you found this case study useful, I have more case studies available at indiakang.com/resources

34

How to Organise a Date Via Text.

You've exchanged numbers and he's asked for a date. You've agreed and he wants to know what day you're free.

Of course, you can't say:
"Pick me up next Wednesday at 7pm sharp."
Even though it's tempting to respond back in this way (and certainly easier) it's not in your interests.

Why not? We don't tell a man what to do. Plus, it would kill the chase.

Here's how to do it:

He says:
"What day is convenient for you?"

You respond:
"Hey, any day next week is good."
Or
"Hey, any day after Wednesday works."

He says:
"Ok how about Thursday?"

You respond:
"Sounds great, see you then."
And that's it. You have a date in the diary for next week. And, you haven't told him what to do. You've been light and breezy.

Let's say you agree to Thursday, only to check your schedule and find you had already agreed to meet the girls for dinner. Do you go back and cancel the Thursday date?

Try not to; if possible change your plans or organise the date around your plans. For example, meet the girls for a drink at 7pm, skip dinner this time and meet your date for 8pm. Everyone's a winner!

What?! You're telling me to cancel plans? It's sisters before misters and I don't cancel plans for any man!

Take a step back and chill out!

I'm not telling you to cancel plans, but a couple of things on this:

You must treat dating like a full time job. Keep this in mind at all times. Dating is a means to an end. No different to finding an actual job.

When you're job-hunting, you free yourself up and make yourself available for interviews. You don't put your life on hold. Neither do you fill up your diary because you never know when you might have an interview.

In this instance, you may tell your friends:

"Hey, would love to meet for drinks. I may have an interview. I'm waiting for confirmation. Can I come back to you?"

In the same way, tell your friends:

"Hey, would love to meet for dinner, I may have a date. Ok if I confirm later?"

This way your friends won't think you've bailed on them. I have to add your true friends will understand. They'll insist you go on the date.

Why? They're your friends and they want to see you happy. When you're dating, play it smart. Make plans which are flexible. Remember, you won't be dating forever.

Why do men ask this? And, why can't he organise the date already? It's only a date!

He's trying. He's doesn't know he's supposed to organise the date, time and arrive with a date plan.

He really doesn't.

He also doesn't want to offend you or come across as controlling and inflexible. He's trying to be polite by asking you to decide the day and time! Cut him some slack. Follow the above script and help him help you.

35

Why Some Men Don't Arrange Date Plans?

This is particularly true at the *Date Zero* stage. The *Date Zero* is the very first date, often only a one or two-hour drink date. The *Date Zero* applies to blind dates, or when you've met online or via a dating app.

If men know your area, they'll have an idea of venues. However, the majority of men will arrive at the date without a set plan.

If they're travelling to you, they probably won't know your area and may need a helping hand.

If he doesn't arrange date plans, does this mean he isn't into me?

At the *Date Zero* stage, it's normal for men to arrive without a date plan, especially if he's travelling to you and doesn't know the area. After the very first date, men normally get planning.

If my date arrives without a date plan, should I ditch him?

If you take this point of view, you'll probably end up ditching 99% of your dates. Don't ditch, follow his lead. Let him arrive and follow the script below.

Meet him at a landmark that's easy for you and direct him subtly. After the introductions, direct him to an area that has bars or cafés. Then wait patiently while he picks one out.

Say something like:

"Sooo, emm... there are a few places to choose from. What do you think?"

Stand still and give him time to process the information and make a decision. Don't rush him.

Once he's had a chance to process, he may say something like:
"What about that bar/coffee shop over there?"

You respond with:
"Sounds great."
Go with whatever he picks or decides.
Easy to be with, hard to get!

36

We Have a Date in the Diary, It's Getting Close and He Hasn't Confirmed! Should I Make Other Plans?

This is very normal. You'll find most men confirm date plans on the actual date day.

The occasional guy will confirm plans a few days in advance, although this is extremely rare. The eager types may confirm on the morning of the actual date, but the vast majority will confirm in the afternoon. For example, if you're meeting at 6.30pm, you'll find he'll get in touch at about 3pm.

When this happens respond back with:
"Great, see you later."

How can you manage this?
You can't control when he gets in touch. He gets in touch when he gets in touch.

What if I spend all this time getting ready and he hasn't confirmed?
Don't get angry. There really is no need. It's a little like getting angry with the weather for being the weather. You can't control when it rains.

What you can do is pack an umbrella!

If you have a date and he cancels but doesn't reschedule, he's a NEXT. Though, of course, if he calls with a good excuse, apologises and reschedules, then give him another chance.

If he keeps rescheduling, he's definitely a NEXT. Either he's not that into you, he's not looking for anything serious or he's not commitment-ready. All of these scenarios equals NEXT.

What if he stands you up?
Again, he's a NEXT.

Should I tell him off?
No, don't bother wasting your time and save your phone bill. He didn't bother to call and cancel, you shouldn't bother either.

Have you been feeling stuck in this area? If you need more help with this dating question, get my free video and other great resources at indiakang.com/resources.

37

What to Do If He Postpones the Date Time?

Let's work through this scenario.

If you were due to meet at 7pm and he says:

"Hey, can we make it 8pm tonight?"

If he postpones once, cut him some slack and tell him

"OK, see you then."

If he keeps postponing, for example, you were due to meet at 7pm, but he changes it to 8pm, and changes it again to 9pm. In this scenario, take a rain check and tell him:

"OK — maybe next time. Have a great evening."

38

We Met Online; I Don't Feel Safe Getting into His Car. Help!

Easy, meet him at a local spot or landmark that is convenient to you and safe, for example a tube stop, a local place of interest or maybe a shop.

You can very playfully say:
"My Mum says I can't get into cars with people who I haven't met. And you know what they say: Mum knows best! How about we meet outside the local Tesco? It's the one on the corner of the High Street and the address is 124 High Street etc."

If he's driving, offers to pick you up but you don't want to disclose your address, playfully say:
"I couldn't possibly get into your car. Blame my Mum; she fills my ears with stranger-danger stories! Honestly, parents! Who'd have them?! Anyway, how about we meet outside the shopping centre or tube station etc."

Give him the address of a local place of interest which is convenient for you and is safe.

PART THREE

IN BETWEEN DATES

1

How to Make Him Pay for Dates

When a man meets his dream girl, the last thing on his mind is splitting the bill. He couldn't care less about paying. It's his pleasure to pay for you.

Think of it this way:

It's like you treating a friend to dinner because she's helped you out. It's your pleasure to pay for her. She helped you through a tough spot, and in return you'd like to treat her. For men, the favour is *you* agreeing to have a date with him.

Remember you're much sought after; a rare find; his dream girl. And you've agreed to a date. What a lucky guy!

As a dating coach, I've noticed how many girls are uncomfortable with the man paying. As soon as the bill arrives, she starts feeling awkward. She feels she's somehow expected to pay. Often, the reality is that, she doesn't know how to receive gracefully. This may sound silly to you: some girls really do have a problem receiving gracefully.

The best advice I can give you, and something that I did myself, is to take a posh or very well-to-do friend out to lunch. Invite her to lunch and tell her it's your treat. When the bill arrives, watch how she conducts herself, watch her hands and her actions. She's effortless because she's so used to people buying her dinner.

Watch how she receives and then emulate her actions. Lunch with this friend won't be cheap, but the lesson will last you a lifetime.

We can't, and we don't, make him pay for dates. If he has a problem paying for a date, chances are he's not that into you, and you can safely turn him down for any future dates. Men who want to date you don't care about the bill!

Would Kate Middleton offer to split the bill with Prince William? Can you imagine Jay-Z asking Beyoncé for her share of the bill?

If you're tempted to pay, or if you're used to paying your own way, leave your purse at home to stop any temptation. When you offer to pay, know that some men find that insulting.

Don't insult him. He's the provider — let him do his job. In the meantime, your job is to learn to receive gracefully and show gratitude.

2

What to Do If He Tries to Prolong the Date

You're on a date and it's going great.

He says any of the following things:

- *"Are you hungry?"*
- *"Would you like to grab a bite?"*
- *"Did you fancy going dancing?"*
- *"Would you like to watch a film?"*

You respond with:

- *"Sounds great, I need to get going. Maybe next time?"*
- *"Sounds great but I have such a busy day tomorrow."*

He may try to prolong the date. It's your job to end the date first. Use the above script and end the date first. Leave him wanting more, not less!

Tone:
Be happy and cheerful.

3

If He Wants to See You Again and You Don't Want Another Date

You can say:
"*Sure, sounds great.*"

He may go home and decide he doesn't want to date you anyway. If he makes contact asking to see you again, you can reply:

"*Hey, sounds great but I'm not really feeling it. Wishing you all the best in your search.*"

Or

"*Hey, it was great to meet you but I'm not feeling any romantic spark. All the best in your search.*"

4

What to Do If Your Date Arrives Late

The majority of my dates, with the exception of my husband, were late.

What can you do?

Don't bother getting mad. Instead, get smart. Buy yourself an e-reader, download some books and use the time to read instead.

Most of my dates were about 40 to 45 minutes late. Don't write them off because they're late for one date. Get smart, and in the beginning cut them some slack and work around it.

What if a guy is consistently ALWAYS late? (Over an hour) Are you allowed to call him out on it in any way? Or, do you say nothing and live with it?

This depends on why he is late. If he traveled three hours to get to you, and got stuck in traffic, in this scenario he's forgiven.

If he's always late without any real excuse. And doesn't call in advance to let you know, then you may want to reconsider.

Weigh up the reasons for his tardiness. If they're plausible forgive him. If he's simply consistently inconsiderate, ditch him!

Have you been feeling stuck in this area? If you need more help with this dating question, get my free video and other great resources at indiakang.com/resources.

5

If He Doesn't Call, Should I Call Him?

The answer to this question will nearly always be 'NO.'

You rarely return his calls and you never call him first.

If he called once, and you missed his call, there is no need to return it. Wait for him to call again. If you have a date in the diary, chances are he'll call again.

We don't know when he'll call. He calls when he calls.

6

How to Navigate the 'Exclusivity Chat'

If you must have the 'exclusivity chat,' (by this I mean, if you don't know where you stand or whether you're even his girlfriend,) then something isn't right.

Normally, this shouldn't need to be discussed. When they want to be with you, they let you know. There's never any doubt in your mind. They tell you constantly. They tell you how they feel and they're always making future plans with you.

Let's say you've been dating three months and you still don't know.

Should you say something?

No, it's better you don't.

The best thing to do is to start pulling back, and, if necessary, start dating others.

Dating others is very powerful. It restores your faith in abundance and gives you options. It also stops you obsessing over any one guy. What an ingenious technique.

How do you know if you're exclusive?

When a man wants to date you, he'll ask for exclusivity fairly early on because he wants you off the dating scene. He doesn't want another man to take you. He wants to ensure you're dating him and him alone; the only way to do this is to become exclusive.

How do you handle exclusivity with men that you meet online?

You don't. You follow his lead. Either he asks for exclusivity or he doesn't. If he doesn't ask, you're both free to date others. May the best man win!

Some men were upset that I was still dating others. In one month, on three separate occasions, men assumed we were exclusive.

If he's unsure, he can ask you. If he hasn't asked, or you're unsure, then assume you're not exclusive. Normally men don't like to assume, they make their feelings very clear.

He may not actually use the exact words "are we exclusive?" Instead, listen out for his vocabulary. Does he call you his girlfriend? Does he tell you that he loves you? How does he introduce you to other people? This all says a lot about what he thinks.

Once exclusive, do you take your dating profile down? What if he hasn't? What should I say if he asks?

Follow his lead. Men normally take down their profiles straight away and without needing to be asked. They're no longer looking, which means there's no need for an online profile. You take your profile down after he's taken down his profile. If he's online and still active, then you continue to stay online and date others.

If he's online, yet hasn't checked his account for the past month or since you became exclusive, chances are he's simply forgotten to remove his profile. In this instance, keep your profile up, simply go inactive too.

You can't ask him to take down his profile. Either he does or he doesn't. Follow his lead and act accordingly.

7

Why Hasn't He Deleted His Online Dating Profile?

If you've only been dating a few weeks, then this isn't a problem. Until you're exclusive, your profile should also stay online.

Do not take down your profile until he has, and then only take it down once you're exclusive. Follow his lead; dating is like a slow dance in which the man leads.

Don't make this into a big deal. Don't stress or wonder what this means. Don't expect him to take down his profile straight away either, the majority of men don't.

Be cool.

His profile may still be online because:

1. He's dating others. He's allowed to and so are you. Until you're exclusive, you're both free to date whomever you like.
2. He may have paid a subscription, and is waiting for his subscription to end before removing his profile.
3. He may have forgotten.

Case Study

I met a guy on a dating website and he's really cute. We've had two dates so far. I noticed he's still logging onto the site every day. What does this mean?

Is he just looking and reading emails? Or does it mean he's seeing others? Plus, if he's online, he can see that I'm logging on as well.

I'm talking to other men, but I'm really not interested in them. How can I bring this up? Can I ask him?

Response:

No, you can't ask him or bring anything up. This scenario should be the other way around. He should wonder why you're still online dating, and he should ponder over what all of this means. Not you.

If he's dating others, then you should follow suit.

Also, you've only had two dates so far, this is nothing. It's very early stages; he may or may not be into you, only time will tell. Some men take down their profiles quickly, whilst others will stay online until their subscription expires. We don't know and we don't care.

Carry on dating others and follow his lead. Don't worry if he sees you're online, let him! If he doesn't want you dating other men, he can always ask for exclusivity.

8

I Checked His Profile, He's Still Active Online. What Should I Do?

Firstly, you should not be checking his profile. You don't want him to think you're spying on him.

If you must spy, create a fake alias, this way you can snoop anonymously. Since you're going to do it anyway, at least stay anonymous. Some dating sites have a functionality that allows you to check other profiles anonymously. You can check this way too.

Don't say *"Hey, I see you're still online. What's the deal with that?"*

It's better to say nothing. Watch and take note of his actions. If he's still online and active, make sure you are too.

Isn't this deceitful?

No, it's smart. It's a little like applying for a job. The interviewer tells you how great and how perfect you are for the job. But you still have two more interview stages to go.

Do you stop looking for other jobs? Or do you think, *"Ok, I may or may not get the job. Who knows? Best to keep applying for other roles."* You never know, you may find a job that is more suited to your skill set, which pays more. Aren't you glad you carried on looking?

At no point, should you tell him to take down his profile. This is similar to telling an organisation to stop recruiting for candidates.

It's the same with dating.

When a man wants to be with you, there is NO doubt in your mind. He'll take his profile down, and he'll ask you to do the same. The search for him is over. He's found his dream girl, and he's not going to let a lesser man take you from him.

If he asks you to take your profile down, and providing you think he may be the one, do it. We don't play games.

PART FOUR

LEADING UP TO AND ONCE EXLCUSIVE

1

If You Can't Make a Date, Can You Suggest Alternative Days?

If he's asked for a particular day three times and each time (by unlucky coincidence) you can't do the day, can you give him an indication of your availability?

Yes, you can. You can drop hints like:

"Thursday is bad because I run then."

He'll know Thursday is a no-go day.

You can also say:

"This week is crazy although next week is better. "

To this he'll ask:

"Ok what days are you free next week?"

You can say:

"Wednesday is a little crazy, and Thursday is my running day. Other than that, I'm free" (let him ask you and figure it out.)

2

Can I Ever Call Him?

Yes, you can: in the following circumstances:

- You're running really late.
- You got stuck at work.
- You were supposed to meet for a date but your boss asked you to stay behind and finish something.
- You're sick and can't make the date.
- Once you're engaged, you can call if some matter needs his attention i.e. he asks you to run an errand and forgets to give you the paperwork. In these instances, you can call and ask where he left the paperwork.

You don't call because you:

- Want to hear his voice.
- Miss him.
- Are needy and clingy.
- You're trying to check up on him.
- He's late picking you up.
- You're bored.
- You're lonely.
- He's out with his friends and you want to know what's going on.
- You want to know if he misses you.
- You want to know if he's thinking about you.

From a practical point of view there will be times when you must call, such as, if you're sick and can't make the date. Even then make sure to end the call first. Don't stay on the phone forever!

3

What If He Thinks I'm Not Interested?

Men who are interested, and I mean really interested, don't scurry away at the first missed call or unanswered text. They find a way to get hold of you. These men don't stop.

Don't be scared to wait before responding to his messages. And only answer if they require a response.

Otherwise simply delete the message, and pretend it never came. This way you'll stop yourself looking at it again and again, obsessing over how to best respond.

Trust and know that, those who want you will find a way. It may not always be immediate. It may take a week or two, sometimes even longer.

That's OK, let him figure it out.

In the meantime, simply go about your business.

Funnily enough being "uninterested" will make him chase harder. One question I'm often asked is *'how come the ones I like don't like me?* And *'how come the ones I don't like, won't leave me alone?'*

This is often the case. Treat the guy you really like as if you don't like him at all.

4

How to Help Him Lead

Your job at the beginning of the courtship is to let him lead and follow his lead. One reason to let him lead, is to work out whether you like the decisions he makes. You get to watch and take notes. Does he make good decisions? Does he put you first when making these decisions?

Most men who want to be with you, will go the extra mile to make you happy. Similarly, they're also listening and taking notes. If you say *"I like Chinese,"* next time he'll book a Chinese restaurant.

Men want to please. They want to make you happy. Your job is to let him, and appreciate his efforts.

What, if you're a fine dining type of girl, and he's into budget basement? In this instance, you either adjust and adapt or stop dating him.

You can't tell him *how* to lead either. He provides what he provides. If it's not satisfactory for you, move on and focus on meeting other men.

You have a choice. You can chill out and follow his lead, or you can fight about having things your way. The choice is yours.

The former is easier, less stressful and makes for a healthy relationship. Understand that telling a masculine energy man what to do will make him feel emasculated. A weaker man may yield, a stronger man will walk away. Masculine energy men don't like playing second fiddle. They may play for a while, but in the long term it won't work.

If, however, *you* want to lead then search for a feminine-energy man; a guy who is happy to follow your lead. Just don't complain that he doesn't make any decisions or isn't able to lead.

5

How to Navigate Cooking

Normally, when a man suggests cooking dinner, this means he's hoping to get lucky.

What he's really thinking is:

"I'll cook her dinner, we can watch a movie and maybe if I'm lucky I might get a cuddle or…"

This doesn't necessarily mean he's only after sex, although sex is probably on his mind.

You can't knock a man for trying!

Some girls consider a man offering to cook as a romantic gesture. They think he's making a lot of effort and trying to impress them. They tell themselves, he must really like me for him to cook.

Don't risk it.

Once you're engaged or married, you can cook dinner every single night. If you're at the very early stages of dating, you're not exclusive and he suggests cooking you dinner and watching a DVD, again you can say:

"Sounds great, but I'm not allowed to go to boys' houses! Open to other suggestions, though."

You're applauding him for his effort, whilst politely saying no. You can use this same response for any invitations over to his house.

What if he really wants to cook for me?

Once again, tell him that it *'Sounds great'* but you'd like to get to know each other first.

When can I cook for him?

There's no rush and not for a while. You can maybe fix him a small snack after you're exclusive. I'm talking a small snack. If he's driven a long distance and you're not eating until later. Something like a bagel, toast, or a sandwich. That's about it. There's no need to worry about his hunger pangs. Remember, he makes the date plans. If he organised a late dinner, he can look after himself until then.

You're not his wife or his mother. Focus on cooking for yourself. Once married you'll do a lot of cooking, enjoy the rest while you can.

Even once you're exclusive, don't worry about impressing him with a three-course meal. Keep it simple and easy. Don't spend all day in the kitchen. There's plenty of time for that once you're married.

He paid for the last three dates. Can I cook to show my appreciation?

No. You don't need to cook for him to show your appreciation. You show your appreciation by turning up, looking hot, being easy to be with and showing gratitude. That's all you need to do.

Don't worry about the cooking. Worry about getting to know each other.

6

Do You Assume You Have a Date on Saturday and Tolerate Late Details?

Try not to see it as 'tolerating.' There's no point getting angry. It's out of your control. As I've mentioned a few times, most men will confirm date plans on the actual day. We don't tell a man how to date. What we can do is manage the situation!

I recommend you get what I call "half-date ready".

Half-date ready is when your dating outfit is all ready to go, and your hair and make-up are nearly done; in essence you are half ready. If he calls and confirms, simply finish applying your make up, pop on your outfit and you're ready to go. In other words, assume your date is happening.

If he doesn't confirm, you can safely press the delete button and cross him off your list of suitors.

Yes, it's always preferable to make other plans, but in reality this isn't always possible. Either call your friends and see if they're free or find a singles event in your local area. Alternatively, simply accept the situation; realise you're going to have your fair share of dating highs and lows, go home and forget about him.

7

I'm on WhatsApp. He Can See When I'm Online. How Do I Navigate?

WhatsApp is the same as chat. On WhatsApp, there are two options as follows:

1. Only check it periodically. This strategy is easier to implement if you have a dating phone, (a cheap handset that you use for dating). This is the number you give to any potential suitors. You can safely turn your dating phone off after the watershed and during the *Dead Zone*. Once your dating days are over, discard your dating phone – any old suitors won't be able to get hold of you. Double whammy.
2. Delete the app. Be smart; don't let a little app get in the way of finding Mr. Right. It's not like it's going to be forever. You can always reinstall the app once you're happily exclusive.

What if I use WhatsApp to connect with all my friends and family?

Use other channels! There's a whole host to choose from. If you're stuck, here are a few to get you started:

- Email (work and or personal)
- Mobile Phone
- Landline

- Skype or any web chat function
- Social media

Be smart when you're dating. Dating is simply a means to an end. I'm not advising you to ignore technology. Rather, these are suggestions to make things a little simpler for yourself.

If you're not happy doing any of the above, the only option is to apply discipline and resist from checking your phone as much.

8

If I Delete His Number How Will I Know It's Him?

If you're tempted to call him, the best preventative measure is to delete his number.

How will you know if he calls?

Easy!

Memorise or write down the last three digits of his number. This way you'll know if it's him who called.

9

Some Other Common Messages and How to Respond

He says:
"Sorry, I'm running late."

You respond:
If you're waiting for him to pick you up and he's running late, there's no need to respond.

When he turns up, he'll probably give his excuse for being late. You can simply say:

"No problem."

Don't make this into a big deal. Act as if nothing has happened. Don't make him feel bad, and don't get all torn up over manners and etiquette. Maybe he got lost. If you live in a big city like London, maybe he got confused on the Underground.

If he's consistently late then you should say something. In the early stages of dating, give him the benefit of the doubt. In the meantime, keep yourself busy. This is a good time to get a Kindle or e-reader and read something positive and uplifting before your date arrives.

He asks:
"Would you like another drink?"

You respond:
"Sure, that'd be great."
Or

"Sounds great, but I better head off. It is a school night!"

If it's not a school night, or, you're meeting him for coffee on a Saturday morning or Sunday afternoon you can say:

"It's been great meeting you. Crazy day today, I better get going."

If he asks:
"Oh really, what have you planned?"

You respond:
"I have plans with the girls and I don't want to be late. Anyway, great meeting you."

He says:
"You're not talking much"

You respond:
"Oh, aren't I? I guess I'm busy listening."

Tone:
Be surprised, like you thought you were talking as much as him.

Why do men ask this?
Well come on, he's used to going on dates where girls talk about themselves incessantly! Now he's come across you. He's realised you're not talking much. You may not be talking, but you are paying attention and taking lots of notes.

He asks:
"When do you want to see me again?"
After the date, he may ask about a follow up date instantly. A short and simple *"Sure, sounds great!"* will more than suffice.

What if you don't want to see him again?

You've been on a date, he really isn't your type, and you don't want to see him again. You can still answer the same as above.

If he asks to see you again, respond with *"Sounds great"* and go off on your merry way. Forget about him until he asks you out again.

If he gets in touch saying:

"Hey beautiful, I had such a great time. Are you free for dinner?"

If you don't want to go, you can respond:

"Hey, great meeting you too. I've been thinking and I really don't feel any spark between us. Wishing you all the best in your search."

He'll get the message.

If, in the beginning you liked him, and now you're unsure, give him another chance. It's only a date. Go out with him. What harm can it do?

Isn't that leading him on?

He may not call you anyway, and he's probably asking out of politeness. You'll have dates where the man will ask for a second date and then nothing. You never hear from him again. Ever.

What happened?

Who knows? It could be anything. Maybe he's dating others and he likes someone else more. Maybe he's not ready for a relationship. Or maybe he was after a short-term fling and realised you're the wrong girl.

It could be any number of reasons. Who cares? If he didn't call you back, he's not that into you.

Period. Over. NEXT.

He says:

"Hey I had a great time meeting you. Look forward to seeing you soon."

If you're dating lots, you'll get used to these types of texts.

Again, you have two choices:

1. You can safely ignore this text. You know he likes you! There's no need for a response. Instead wait for him to ask for another date, or wait for him to call.
2. You can respond with a simple smiley face.

Why do men do this?
Simple, they're thanking you for the date, that's all. There's no need to respond to every single text either.

He asks
"What are you up to?"
In this instance, it depends why he sent the text.

If you're newly dating and there's no date in the diary, ignore this text. This text means nothing. He's probably bored.

If you're exclusive and dating for months, it's unlikely he'll send this type of message.

If he calls and asks:
"What have you been up to/what are you doing now?"

You can respond with:
"Oh, you know the usual; this and that."

He asks:
"Do you want to come over? Maybe grab a pizza and watch a movie?"
Or any other variants that involves you going over to his place.

You respond:
"Sounds great but I couldn't possibly, I'm not allowed to go to boys' houses!"

Why do men ask this?
Bless him; he's trying his luck. Can you blame him? Nice try, and the answer in the beginning will always be *'no.'*

Case Study

I met a guy online. We've spoken on the phone a couple of times. We're yet to meet although he seems nice enough. A couple of things were kind of odd though.

He asked questions about my past relationships, whether I'd ever married. He also asked if I liked children, whether I'm religious and what my deal breakers are. Then he said, how I look beautiful on my profile picture. He ended by saying we might hit it off, as it could be love at first sight.

What do you think of these questions? Should I meet him?

Response

For a start, this guy hasn't even asked you for a date. At this stage, you've only spoken on the phone. If he asks for a date, sure, meet him for a coffee. Agreeing to meet for a coffee doesn't constitute a legal and binding lifelong commitment.

In terms of his questions, these are pretty normal. He's asking questions as a way to get to know you better. At this stage, don't read too much into anything. Thank him for the nice compliment, and watch his actions. If he continues to call, asks heaps of questions, yet never asks for a date, stop taking his calls. Chances are he's a time waster.

If you found this case study useful, I have more case studies available at indiakang.com/resources

PART FIVE

HANDLING QUESTIONS AROUND MARRIAGE, CHILDREN AND PAST RELATIONSHIPS.

1

Questions Related to Marriage

In the beginning *all* questions related to marriage are traps. When I say trap, I don't mean men ask these types of questions on purpose or he's trying to trap you. He can ask; doesn't mean you should answer.

Here's how to safely navigate:

"What do you think about marriage?"
"I haven't really thought about it. How about you?"

"Do you want to get married?"
"I haven't really thought about it. How about you?"

"Are you looking for marriage?"
"Give me a chance; I've only started dating! How about you?"

"Are you looking to settle down?"
"It depends on the person really. How about you?"

"Do you believe in marriage?"
I guess it's OK. Why? Do you believe in marriage?

What if he brings it up?

Let him, and he probably will. Some men will bring up marriage on the first or second date. He can talk about marriage, you don't reciprocate. You don't need to answer, and you can safely dodge the question by asking him the same questions back.

Don't get frazzled by these questions either. Most men ask the same questions. Get ahead of the game and practice the answers in this book.

Why do men ask this?

He thinks these are normal questions to ask. A little like going for a job interview and getting asked *"what you do for fun?"*

What you do for fun has nothing to do with your ability to do the job; they're simply trying to find out more about you. That's all!

2

He Asks "Do You Want Children?"

You respond:
"Emmm... (small pause) children can be cute. My niece is so adorable. How about you?"

Tone:
Respond as if you've never given this topic any thought. You've never thought about children ever. Even if you have, you still mustn't say anything. Not yet anyway.

If, however you don't want children, in this instance you can tell him. Simply say *"No I don't want children."*

Why do men ask this question?
This question also falls into the 'trap' category. Men aren't deliberately trying to trick you. Again, it's nothing sinister. Once again, in the beginning there's no need to answer.

Let him talk about how many children he wants, and the cute names he's going to call them. In the meantime, all you need to do is smile and keep quiet.

Don't worry; yes, you will be able to talk about children, just not yet.

"What do you want to name your kids?"
Again another 'trap' question. He can talk about children, marriage and the future all he wants but you can't. I know — double standards. Sorry, that's just the way it is.

You can answer as follows:

"Emm I've not really thought about it. How about you?"

Answer the question in a nonchalant and effortless way, and change the subject.

Why do men ask this?

Men think about children. The reason we fall in love is because our human instinct wants us to reproduce. By mating we continue the human species. When a man meets you, he's already worked out whether he thinks you'd be a good gene carrier. That said, in the early stages of dating, talking about marriage and children might scare him off. Use the above responses to safely navigate these questions.

3

Questions About Past Relationships

The majority of men will ask questions about your past relationships. It's normal; again, they're trying to work you out.

Be careful when answering any questions about past relationships. As always, in the beginning keep this vague, mainly because at this stage it's none of his business.

As you get to know each other better, you can open up a little more. That said, don't say how your previous relationships were amazing, and how you were so happy with boyfriend number two. Telling him this will make him feel uneasy, and he may start to compare himself to your old boyfriends. It's also not good for him to 'imagine' you with other men.

For all these reasons, keep these answers very vague.

Here are a few ways to navigate:

"When was your last relationship?"
"Emm, a couple of years ago."
"A while ago."
"I've been single for a while."
"About a year ago."

"How many boyfriends have you had?"
"You're so nosey! Right, from now on I'm going to call you Mr. Nosey." (Say this in a very playful way, almost pretend you're insulted but of course you're not.)
Or you can shrug it off, there's no need to tell him anything. Simply say:
"Past relationships are so boring; let's talk about something else."

This way you haven't answered the question, you're polite, and swerved around this delicate trap-ridden topic.

What if you're recently single or divorced?
Tell him the truth. Again, don't elaborate.
If he asks about your divorce, simply say:
"I've been divorced a couple of months. I guess we weren't compatible."
Then change the subject.
Answer honestly without oversharing because it's none of his business.

What if he talks about his ex?
Let him, he can talk all he wants, you don't need to reciprocate.

What if he badmouths his ex?
Some men will bad-mouth their ex-partners, others won't. Don't judge him based on his words, judge him on his actions. If he treats you mean, then his ex-girlfriend probably had a lucky escape. If he treats you well, give him a chance.

Who knows — maybe she really was an ogre! Time will tell, for now watch and take notes. What have you got to lose? You'll find out if he's a good or bad guy soon enough.

If, however, he continuously talks about what a 'bad' boy he is, how he gets bored quickly with the same girl and can't remain faithful – in this case it might be prudent to move on.

Why do men ask this?
They are working out whether you're a keeper. Whatever you do, don't give him a report on your past relationships. Don't talk about how you dumped your last boyfriend, how you're still in love with your crush from school, or how you find break ups painful.

You wouldn't turn up at a job interview and drone on about how awful your last job was, or how much you hated your boss.

This is interview suicide. Plus, for all you know, this guy may know your ex. Who knows!

Have you been feeling stuck in this area? If you need more help with this dating question, get my free video and other great resources at indiakang.com/resources.

4

How to Navigate the Ex

All discussions around the ex are a pain. Your ex, his ex... it can all get very draining. The exes well and truly belong in the past. Keep them there. Focus on the present and put your energy on dating your current suitor. Sometimes this is easier said than done. You can't control your ex and you can't control what they'll do. Do the best you can. In the meantime, here are some ways to get you started.

"He always talks about his ex!"
If you think he's still in love with his ex, then NEXT. If he wants to be with his ex, he will. There is nothing stopping him from getting her back. If this is what he wants, stand aside, wish them both the best, and let him go.

Should I mention my ex?
No! Don't talk about your ex.
The less you know about each other's exes the better, otherwise you'll start imagining all sorts of things. And you'll drive yourself crazy.
I have one friend who made a pact with her husband to never discuss their exes. Great pact! They're married. They don't need to know about each other's exes. All they care about is their current relationship. Sure, they both dated, but it was in the past!

"I can't date a guy, who won't accept I'm friends with my ex!"
Be prepared to stay single, or be prepared to have arguments about your ex with your current boyfriend. Most men don't want to

know about your ex because they don't want to 'imagine' you with someone else. It works both ways. Do you really want to meet his ex? What if she was some long-legged, blonde bombshell? You'd start comparing. Doesn't sound like a whole lot of fun.

Don't force your ex and your current boyfriend together either.

"He's always talking about how his ex-girlfriends looked like supermodels"

Good for him! He clearly has good taste. If his past relationships were so great, and his ex-girlfriend was so hot, why aren't they still together? If he wants to date a supermodel, he will. If he wants to date you, he will. It's nothing for you to worry about. Either he likes your look or he doesn't.

"My ex and I are very good friends."

Good for you. Now focus on your current relationship.

"His ex is always contacting him!"

Do you blame her? She's probably realised what a great catch he is. Too bad for her. She had her chance. As long as he's not calling her, you're OK. Remember if he wanted to be with her, he would!

"Surely if he loved me he wouldn't talk to her?"

You can't tell a man what to do. Normally, if he sees it bothers you, he'll stop. But don't make it into a big drama. Don't say anything at all, just be quiet. She'll stop soon enough.

"Did he love her more than he loves me?"

Who knows? The point is he doesn't love her anymore, just like you no longer love your ex. Imagine if you'd married your ex? Thankfully you didn't. Phew. Right?

"What if I'm still in love with my ex?"

Unfortunately, he's not in love with you. If he wanted you, he'd be with you. Harsh I know, but it's the truth. Don't waste time on men who don't want you.

The best way to move on from an ex is as follows:

1. Have a purge and remove every single item that reminds you of him. This includes photos, cards, cutesy notes, his number, any gifts he gave you. If he gave you expensive gifts, sell them. The only time to keep his gifts, is if looking at them evokes bad memories. In this instance, keep the item as a way of reminding you what a lucky escape you had. If looking at his gifts brings back fond memories: bin, recycle, sell or give it away. The reason to purge is to do with a chemical called oxytocin. Oxytocin bonds the female to the male. Oxytocin is powerful. Every time you look, touch, feel, smell or think of him, this chemical is released into your body, thereby bonding you to him long after he's gone. This is one reason girls stay with men who are no good for them. It's not love; it's science.
2. Date other men immediately. Even if you don't feel like it, at least sign up to some singles events. It doesn't matter if the event is a few weeks away, sign up anyway and while you're at it create an online dating profile too. Dating others is the very last thing you'll want to do, which is precisely why you must.
3. If you need a short holiday by all means take one, make sure to start the dating process first. No matter how small the effort is, do something to meet men. Anything. Even if all you do, is get dressed up and go to a coffee shop. Do it. It's a start.

"His ex is a friend of mine"
Unfriend her pronto and don't go out of your way to socialize together.

"My ex is a Facebook friend"
Unfriend him.

"My ex keeps trying to get me back"
It all depends on who broke up with whom, why, and of course whether you want him back.

If he broke up with you, move on.

If he broke up with you on your birthday, Valentine's Day, Christmas or some other significant date, never take him back. No matter how much he pleads. Do not take him back.

Can I stay friends with my ex?
Yes, you can, however don't focus on the ex. Don't you have dates to set up and a future to build with Mr. Right?

On that note, when is your next singles party?

He asks:
"What happened with your ex?"

Respond in any of the following ways:
"It was so long ago, I can hardly remember."
"Nothing much."
"Talking about exes is so boring don't you think? Let's play I spy."

Tone:
Nonchalant, like you really can't remember. Anyway, who cares about the ex?

PART SIX

SOME COMMON *RULES* FURTHER EXPLAINED

1

Wednesday for Saturday and the Three Day *Rule*

If he doesn't ask for a Saturday date by Wednesday, make other plans. If he asks on Thursday, it's too late and you must politely decline.

You can say something along the lines of:
"Sounds great! Shame I have other plans."
Say this cheerfully and with a huge smile on your face.

If he asks any later than Wednesday, you can't go. Simply turn him down very nicely. It's much better you don't have a Saturday night date. Don't make excuses for him, even if he is your dream guy.

Men are smart and they're also problem solvers. By turning him down, he'll start asking sooner.

2

How to Navigate Last-Minute Dates

He asks any of the following:

- *"Hey, are you free tonight?"*
- *"Hey, do you fancy sushi tomorrow?"*
- *"Hey, fancy meeting up later?"*
- *"Hey, are you free tomorrow?"*

You respond:
"Sounds great, shame I already have plans, sorry. Maybe another time,"

Why do men do this?
He's being lazy, and he's been spoilt by other girls who have happily accepted last-minute dates. It doesn't make him bad. If he can get away with asking at the last minute, he will. You don't need to accept though.

By turning him down, he'll realise he needs to start asking earlier. He'll start to ask on Monday for a date on Saturday. Hold your ground and turn down any last minute dates.

Have you been feeling stuck in this area? If you need more help with this dating question, get my free video and other great resources at indiakang.com/resources.

3

How to Make Him Travel to You

He says:
"Maybe we could meet for a drink sometime? Let me know when you're next in my neck of the woods."

Or he may say:
"There's a great pizza place next to my work. Maybe we could check it out sometime?"

You can respond with:
"Sure"
And then leave it.

Of course, you NEVER travel to him; you don't catch trains and buses to be near him. It doesn't matter how cute he is.

Neither do you make it easy for him to date you. Don't try and justify it by saying you wanted to go there anyway. Yes, by all means check out that part of town, do it on your own or with your friends. Don't make excuses to meet halfway or travel to him.

If he wants to date you, he'll happily come to you.

But he lives so far away!

Even better! Don't worry, for the right girl – men will travel for hours.

Don't make excuses for him.

4

How to Successfully Navigate the Meeting-Halfway *Rule*

The *Meeting-Halfway Rule* is commonly misunderstood. Here are a couple of ways to safely navigate it.

If he says:
"Hey, let me know when you're next in my area?"

You can say:
"Sure, will do."

Of course, you won't. Simply end the call politely. If he wants to date you, he has your number!

If he suggests meeting near a place that's closer to him than it is to you, again, turn him down.

You can say:
"It's sooooo far. Maybe next time."

Or you can say:
"I thought you were a gentleman. Are you really going to make me travel all that way?"

Either he'll laugh, lose interest, or suggest somewhere closer to you. Trust that whatever response you get, is the right response.

Why do men suggest meeting halfway?
He likes you, but he's not crazy about you. If he asks you to

meet him halfway, you can safely assume he is not into you. For him, you're not worth the time and investment.

Meeting halfway requires less effort.

For the right girl, a man will travel miles, he'll even catch planes. Keep turning him down for any requests to meet halfway. Either you're worth the effort or you're not.

Another way to navigate the *Meeting-Halfway Rule*:

He says:
"How about we meet on Junction 2 off the motorway?"

You can either delete this text or respond with:
"So sorry, maybe another time."

If he says:
"OK let me know when you're free!"

You can say:
"Sure"
And say nothing else. If he wants to date you, he'll get in touch.

How to navigate living in a big city, and meeting men after work who suggest you travel to them

He says:
"How about we meet tomorrow 6pm outside Piccadilly Circus?"

You say:
"Sounds great. Tomorrow is cool. Piccadilly Circus will be difficult."

He may say:
"Ok can you meet later?"

In this case respond with:
"Maybe next time, have a great evening." (NO! You cannot do later and travel to him.)

If he says:
"Ok what works for you?"

You can say:
"I can meet tomorrow after work near Waterloo" (choose a convenient location).

You may have to turn him down a couple of times before he figures it out. Be polite and cordial at all times and see what happens.

Case Study

My boyfriend and I have been dating three months or so and we agreed to go bowling on Wednesday. The bowling alley is based centrally. He suggested we meet at the bowling alley; it's about a 30-minute journey for both of us. Can I meet him there or does he have to come to me, pick me up to take me to the bowling alley?

You don't travel to him. In this scenario since he's planned activities centrally then yes, meet him there. If you prefer to stay in your area only, don't agree to anything outside your area.

You can say:
"Bowling sounds fun. I wondered whether we could do something local. I have a crazy day tomorrow, what do you think?"
This way he'll come to you.

In the bowling example, he doesn't need to come to you to accompany you to the activity. The *Meeting-Halfway Rule* is, where, for example he lives east, you live west and he wants to meet centrally because it's convenient for him. If he wants to meet centrally because you've agreed to an activity, meet him centrally or don't agree to the activity.

Case Study

I have a *Date Zero* with this guy I met at a speed dating event last week. He suggested coffee and asked how Thursday was for me, which I agreed to. He suggested meeting halfway. I said I have a party to go to after work in the city. He said he will work around my schedule, travel to me, and then asked what time I could make it. I responded asking *'what time did he have in mind?'*

Then he wrote, since I'm working and have a party, I should organise the time for our date.

How should I reply? Since he's travelling to me, I can meet him any time in the evening.

Response

Well done! This is exactly the way to behave. Respond nicely and say, *"yes"* to anything reasonable. Don't travel to him or meet halfway. In this instance, he's travelling to you, he's accommodating your party, and he's trying to pin you down. You can respond with:

"Any time after 7pm works great."

You're light and breezy, easy to be with, yet hard to get. Follow the man's lead. You did a great job!

But shouldn't he decide the time?

In this example it's OK to help him out a little. You only stated *"any time after 7pm."* He is still making the final decision. He picks the time after 7pm. If he says 10pm, you can politely decline. A 10pm coffee date is too late.

5

How to Navigate the Dead Zone

The *Dead Zone* is a marvellous place. It starts at Friday 6pm and ends on Sunday 6pm.

It's like a mini holiday, especially if you've been dating all week. This is how it works:

If you have a scheduled date in the diary

If he texts, wait before responding. Don't text back immediately. If he calls, pick up the phone because he may be calling about date plans. Basically, respond providing there's a scheduled date in the diary.

If you don't have a scheduled date in the diary

In this instance ignore all texts and calls. If you have a dating phone, turn it off or change the ringer to vibrate or silent. Any messages can wait until after the *Dead Zone*. No date means he does NOT exist.

What if he calls before 6pm on Friday and we don't have a date?

Ignore and respond back after the *Dead Zone*.

If he texts at 5.59pm and you have a date on that day?

Respond, wait a few minutes if you can.

What happens on bank holidays and public holidays?

The *Dead Zone* extends to public holidays. The only time to respond during the *Dead Zone,* is if there's a confirmed date in the diary.

6

What Is the Date Zero?

The *Date Zero* is the very first face-to-face date with someone you met on an online dating site or mobile app. If you met a guy down the pub who asked for your number, this isn't classified as a *Date Zero*. You've already met.

The *Date Zero* lasts no more than two hours, although it can be shorter. The idea is that you're in and out within two hours maximum. No messing about. No six-hour dates. There's little investment in terms of time. You meet him, have a coffee or a drink, end the date first and you're gone.

The *Date Zero* can be any day except Saturday evening. For example, you can have a *Date Zero* on Saturday morning, Saturday afternoon, and Saturday early evening. You can meet at 4pm on a Saturday, have a quick drink, make your excuses and you're off.

The reason we stay away from Saturday night dates is because there are certain expectations associated with Saturday night. It's harder to make your excuses after two hours.

That said, if you haven't worked out how to navigate setting up a *Date Zero,* (which takes some practice) and you end up on a Saturday night *Date Zero*, don't drive yourself crazy or panic. Don your heels, best dating outfit, turn up, and end the date after two hours. Get it over and done with. It's only a date!

The first two or three dates can be any day. After that he must ask for Saturday night. You'll find that any man who wants to be with you, will start asking for Saturday night pretty much straight away. Why? Come on, he's found his dream girl; there's no one else he'd rather spend Saturday night with! Men who want to date you, want to take you out on Saturday night. However, if he works Saturday nights then Fridays and Sundays are OK.

Most men won't make it past one date, so you'll have lots of *Date Zeros*! Keep setting them up, they help you practice dating and reflect on your deal breakers.

If I have a Saturday date and he hasn't confirmed plans, should I make other plans and stop answering his messages?

In this example, take his call. Providing he booked you three days in advance, take the call; he might be calling to confirm the date.

7

Bookmarking

What is *Bookmarking*?

Bookmarking is when a guy will ask if you're free for a date but doesn't follow up. He might say: *"Are you free on Thursday?"* After this you hear nothing more. He's *Bookmarked* you for Thursday, just in case another plan falls through.

I'm confused! I thought we had to discourage *Bookmarking*, and be stricter if plans are not firm three days beforehand?

If he's booked you for dinner on Saturday, chances are he'll confirm the time and place on that day. In my experience, most men confirm date plans on the day of the date. Some confirm in the morning, while others may confirm a couple of days before.

If he asks for dinner on Thursday, yet doesn't confirm any plans at all, then forget about him! If he texts the next day with some lame excuse, again, forget about him.

PART SEVEN

ODDS AND ENDS BUT STILL IMPORTANT

1

Why Do Men Only Talk About Themselves?

This is normal, and you'll find most men will happily talk about themselves. This is great for you as:

1. You don't have to say much. What a great way to retain the mystery! It's effortless, all you have to do is turn up, look great, and let him talk.
2. You get to listen and take important notes. For example, if he says, *"I'm a big loser, I can't find a job and every time I do, I get sacked."* That's important information, right? Let him talk and don't try to fill in the gaps.

I thought men didn't like to talk?
Generally, they don't. The reason men don't like to talk is evolutionary. Their primary role was to hunt. If he talked, the prey would hear him coming, which meant no dinner for you. This is different in the early stages of dating. In the beginning, he's trying to impress you.

Shouldn't he try to get to know me?
He will, and there's plenty of time for him to get to know you. Remember, most men won't make it past the first couple of dates. Do you really want random men knowing personal information about you? Of course you don't. Don't complain about men talking so much. This doesn't make him a narcissist either.

Why do men do this?

He's telling you what he's got to offer. In essence, he's pitching the goods.

Have you been feeling stuck in this area? If you need more help with this dating question, get my free video and other great resources at indiakang.com/resources.

2

Men Who Ask Interview-type Questions

Some men will ask interview-type questions, such as:

- *"What are your dreams/hopes/regrets?"*
- *"What character traits annoy you in people?"*
- *"What are you looking for in a soul mate?"*
- *"Do you believe in love at first sight?"*

Any of the above you can answer with:

"Now, there's a question!"
Say this in a friendly way and change the subject.

Otherwise you can say:
"So many questions! Anyway, did you watch X on TV last night?"

Why do men do this?
Again, it's no different to those pointless interview questions. If he asks annoying questions, deflect them as I've shown and remember to smile.

3

I Don't Need a Man

OK, so stay single.

"I can do things for myself." I hear you say.

I'm pretty sure you can. Having a man doesn't mean you stop doing things for yourself. He is simply the cherry on top.

4

The Dating Phone

You should have a dating phone separate from your personal phone. Give out your dating phone number to whoever asks, and keep the two phones separate! This gives you an extra degree of privacy, security and protection.

You can also turn the phone off after the watershed, which means no booty calls and no need to worry about men calling late at night. If they call late, they get your voicemail. And, you won't get woken up at 3am, with silly texts sent by men, who have nothing better to do.

Be smart, invest in a cheap handset.

5

What to Do If You're Propositioned?

If he asks:
"Are you up for something less serious?"
"Do you fancy having some no-strings-attached fun?"
Unless you're looking for 'fun' the answer is, *"thanks, but no thanks."*
Be flattered, don't get annoyed and all flustered.
Don't say anything like:
"How dare you!"
Or
"Who do you think you are?!"

Smile and tell him:
"Sorry, you've got the wrong girl."
You can also end the date soon, no need to stick around. Thank him for the date and head home.
That's all you need to do.
If you're dating, chances are you will get propositioned at least once.
If you keep attracting men who are only after one thing, time to take a look within.
Like attracts like; if this reoccurs multiple times, then there is something in you which is attracting this type of attention. Is it what you're wearing? Check your dating profile pictures. Are you maybe revealing too much skin? Are you posing in a suggestive manner? If you're not sure – ask a trusted friend for their opinion.

6

What Are You Up To?

You're both dating for a month or so, and he asks:
"What are you up to?"
Since, you're not doing anything special, how do you answer while retaining mystery?

You can say any of the following in a very playful way:

- *"Emmm... you know this and that."*
- *"It's top secret, if I told you I may have to kill you, and I don't want to do that!"*
- *"Emmm... just the usual."*

If he asks:
"Like what?"

You can say:

- *"You know, a bit of this and a bit of that."*
- *"You know... the usual things."*

If he asks:
"What are the usual things?"

You can say:
"Ohh can't tell you, it's top secret."
Keep your responses really light and playful, and laugh a lot.

7

You vs. Non-*Rules* Girls

As a *Rules Girl*, you'll get asked some of the following questions. They're completely normal. Men aren't used to meeting a *Rules Girl,* and are often baffled by the way we conduct and hold ourselves.

You're completely different from your non-*Rules* sisters, which means you stand out from the crowd.

Here are some other commonly asked questions:

He asks:
"Are you even interested?"

You respond:
"I'm enjoying getting to know you."
"I certainly wouldn't waste your time."

Normally when you respond as above, he'll start feeling relieved. Make sure you say this sincerely.

Why do men ask this?
They've never met a *Rules Girl*, and they can't work out if you're even interested in them. Other girls make their affections known. They may post status updates on their Facebook saying "so in love". Or they send text messages so he knows how she feels.

When men start backing off, there's a false belief it's because you didn't tell him how you felt. This is completely false. Some girls think if they talk feelings, it'll bring him closer. It may have the opposite effect and drive him away.

Why?

You're no longer a challenge, and men love a challenge.

He asks:

"What's with the mystery?"

You respond:

"What do you mean?"

Say this playfully, like you don't have a clue what he is talking about.

Why do men ask this?

They're intrigued and they're totally hooked. You don't say much and you rarely text or call. They can't work you out!

He asks:

"How come you don't call?"

As a *Rules Girl*, men will ask *"why do you never call?"* Act dumb, and playfully say any of the following:

You respond:

- *"Don't I? I've been busy. I promise to try harder."*
- *"Guess I've just been busy!"*
- *"Funny you say that, I was thinking about calling you!"* (Of course, you weren't but — hey — a little white lie never hurt anyone.)

Again, act a little surprised, as if you really don't have a clue what he's talking about.

Why do men ask this?

All other girls call and text. His last girlfriend probably called him all the time and you won't. He's a little confused. Yes, you can call occasionally. Even then there won't be any need.

Why?

He's either always calling or getting in contact via text or email. If you prefer calls, stop responding to texts, email, and other types of chat-apps. The reason he's always trying to reach you is because you're always on his mind! He's always thinking about you. And, you'll discover that he's always talking about you too.

He says:
"There's something different about you."

You respond:
"Oh really, aren't girls all the same?"
Or
"Oh really, how so?"

When you say this, act a little surprised and baffled. What could he possibly mean?

Why do men ask this?
Again, they can't work you out. You'll get used to hearing this. They're right. There is something different about you. You're not like the others. It's a good thing. Keep it up.

Case Study One

I met a guy via a mobile app. He wrote saying: *"I'd like to talk and text for a while, get to know you and work out if you are worth meeting."*

I stopped talking to him immediately. He'll never know how great I am now! Did I do the right thing?

Response

Jeez! He certainly has a way with words. Bless him. Maybe he's not great at expressing himself, or maybe he doesn't realise his words can be offensive. He may or may not call. If he calls, sure pick up. What have you got to lose? It's only ten minutes and you never know what could happen. He could be a loser, or he may be fantastic. Either way, it's only ten minutes of your time.

Yes, he could have worded his message better but unfortunately he didn't. Give him a chance and see what happens.

Case Study Two

On Sunday, I registered with an online-dating site and received some messages. One guy winked, which I ignored. He then emailed the following exchange.

Him (on Sunday morning): *"Good morning. I'm Evan."*

Me (about 8 hours later): *"Hi. I'm Lucy."*

Him (the next day): *"Lovely to meet you. How are you doing?"*

Me (this morning): *"Busy day, so it went very fast! How was yours?"*

Him (one hour later): *"Busy as well. I manage a sports shop."*

Me (after a further hour): *"A sports shop sounds busy! Does a manager of a sports shop need to be sporty?"*

Him (after just 10 minutes): *"Yes it helps! How about you? Are you sporty?"*

This will be our fourth email and he hasn't asked for my number. I registered for online sites in the past and ended up with endless emailing. I don't want to repeat this behaviour. I also got a lot of winks and likes, which I've ignored.

Can I ignore his last email?

Response

Yes, ignore his last email. Also, ignore any winks, pokes, likes, waves or whatever the function is on that particular dating site. You're only interested in men who take time to read and write something about your profile.

In this instance, there was no need to respond to his first message. His first email is a generic cut-and-paste email. He mentioned nothing about your profile. Only respond if he mentions something about your profile.

He probably sends the same, *'Hi I'm Evan'* email to every other girl on the site. It takes no effort on his part and now you're replying to him. Don't bother.

Also, you responded in the morning. Aren't you at work? Why are you checking your online dating emails in the morning? Leave online-dating to the evening.

The best way to navigate online-dating is to online date three days a week, for example Tuesday, Thursday and Sunday. This way you're not constantly online. Log in on these days, commit to an hour per session, read the messages and reply to whoever asks for your number, after that log off.

This way you get to have a life. On the remaining days, go to the gym, speed dating, singles events or simply stay in, recuperate and watch TV.

Case Study Three

This guy keeps texting me. He texts every evening with general chit chat. He'll ask about what I'm doing or he'll talk about the weather. We've been texting for a week.

Is he a time waster? Should I stop responding?

Response

Yes, he's a time waster! Stop responding, there was no need to respond to his first text either. Delete all his messages and delete his number. He has your number. He can call you.

Case Study Four

My on-and-off boyfriend keeps breaking up with me and coming back.

Response
NEXT!

If he keeps breaking up and then tries to get you back - he is a NEXT.

If you let him, this guy will waste months or even years of your time.

Stop dating him. He may try and get you back, that doesn't mean *you* take him back.

You're the one in control. He can only come back if you let him.

About India Kang

India Kang is a dating and relationship coach for women, a relationship expert for Match UK, former advice columnist, and a *Rules*-certified dating coach. *The Rules* is the cult dating manual by the authors Ellen Fein and Sherrie Schneider.

She is also the author to *'How to Date–Single Girls' Dating Manual'*. And, she is regularly featured in the media, press, radio and TV.

India comes from a classic advertising background, having worked for many of the top ten global advertising agencies including Ogilvy Worldwide, Publicis, G2, EHS Brann on global campaigns for Shell, BT, Diageo, Vodafone, Royal Mail, Hewlett Packard, Cisco, 3, British Gas to name a few

India is married and currently lives and works in Solihull.